LAWS AND LEGISLATION SERIES

A COMPARATIVE ANALYSIS OF DISABILITY LAWS

LAWS AND LEGISLATION SERIES

Clean Diamond Trade Act
James T. Williams (Editor)
2009. ISBN: 978-1-60741-111-6

Revisiting and Evaluating the Congressional Review Act
Katherine R. Williamson (Editor)
2009. ISBN: 978-1-60692-687-1

State Secrets Protection Act
Lara H. Nellington (Editor)
2009. ISBN: 978-1-60692-711-3

Restoring the Rule of Law
Patricia V. Barkley (Editor)
2009. ISBN: 978-1-60692-970-4

Federal Torts Reform, Claims and Liability
Ben V. Colligan (Editor)
2009. ISBN: 978-1-60692-989-6

Contemporary Perspectives on Legal Regulation of Sexual Behavior: Psycho-legal Research and Analysis
Monica K. Miller (Editor)
2009. ISBN: 978-1-60741-161-1
(Hardcover)

Contemporary Perspectives on Legal Regulation of Sexual Behavior: Psycho-legal Research and Analysis
Monica K. Miller (Editor)
2009. ISBN: 978-1-60876-779-3
(Online Book)

Abortion: Legislative and Legal Issues
Kevin G. Nolan (Editor)
2010. ISBN: 978-1-60741-522-0

Copyright Law and A Brief Look at the Google Library Project
Brett D. Rhodes (Editor)
2010. ISBN: 978-1-60741-871-9

Antitrust Modernization
Luigi Ferrigno (Editor)
2010. ISBN: 978-1-60741-805-4

Copyright and the Orphan Works Issue
Andrew D. Owens (Editor)
2010. ISBN: 978-1-60741-721-7

How Laws are Made in the U.S.A.
Helen Maes (Editor)
2010. ISBN: 978-1-60876-142-5

How Pretrial Publicity Affects Juror Decision Making and Memory
Christine L. Ruva
2010. ISBN: 978-1-61668-328-3
(Softcover)

How Pretrial Publicity Affects Juror Decision Making and Memory
Christine L. Ruva
2010. ISBN: 978-1-61668-587-4
(Online Book)

American Recovery and Reinvestment Act: History, Overview, Impact
Paul G. Tellis (Editor)
2010. ISBN: 978-1-61668-355-9
(Hardcover)

American Recovery and Reinvestment Act: History, Overview, Impact
Paul G. Tellis (Editor)
2010. ISBN: 978-1-61668-390-0
(Online Book)

Judge Sonia Sotomayor: Selected Options
Patrick K. Reed (Editor)
2010. ISBN: 978-1-60876-759-5

Congressional Compromise: Amendments between the House and the Senate
Julio D. Nachtrieb and Liam J. Cadriel (Editors)
2010. ISBN: 978-1-60741-796-5
(Hardcover)

Congressional Compromise: Amendments between the House and the Senate
Julio D. Nachtrieb and Liam J. Cadriel (Editors)
2010. ISBN: 978-1-61668-884-4
(Online Book)

Judge Sonia Sotomayor: Selected Options
Patrick K. Reed (Editor)
2010. ISBN: 978-1-60876-759-5

A Comparative Analysis of Disability Laws
John R. Vaughn
2010. ISBN: 978-1-60741-536-7

LAWS AND LEGISLATION SERIES

A COMPARATIVE ANALYSIS OF DISABILITY LAWS

JOHN R. VAUGHN

Nova Science Publishers, Inc.
New York

LIBRARY OF CONGRESS CATALOGING-IN-PUBLICATION DATA

Vaughn, John R.
A comparative analysis of disability laws / John R. Vaughn.
p. cm.
Includes bibliographical references and index.
ISBN 978-1-60741-536-7 (hardcover)
1. People with disabilities--Legal status, laws, etc.--United States. 2. Convention on the Rights of Persons with Disabilities and Optional Protocol (2007) 3. International and municipal law--United States. I. Title.
KF480.V38 2009
342.7308'7--dc22

2009034181

Published by Nova Science Publishers, Inc. ✝ *New York*

CONTENTS

PREFACE

The purpose of this book is to help the National Council on Disability (NCD), and others, better understand how the Convention on the Rights of Persons with Disabilities, if ratified by the United States, might impact U.S. disability laws by examining the degree to which U.S. law is consistent with the CRPD. The book endeavors to analyze the issue in the way a treaty monitoring body would - to see if any area within federal law contravenes the Convention and/or whether there are gaps where legislation or practice might be introduced or reformed to ensure compliance. This book also identifies several CRPD articles that illustrate significant gaps between United States disability laws and the Convention.

Chapter 1

EXECUTIVE SUMMARY

This paper is geared toward understanding the degree to which U.S. law (in form, spirit, and practice) is consistent with the CRPD. Because any comparison is of necessity at times between "apples and oranges," the paper endeavors to analyze the issue in the way a treaty monitoring body would - to see if any area within federal law contravenes the Convention and/or whether there are gaps where legislation or practice might be introduced or reformed to ensure compliance. The paper finds that, as a general matter, the aims of the CRPD are consistent with U.S. disability law. For the majority of articles, U.S. law can be viewed as either being of a level with the mandates of the Convention or capable of reaching those levels either through more rigorous implementation and/or additional actions by Congress. However, this paper also identifies several CRPD Articles that illustrate significant gaps between United States disability laws and the Convention.

PURPOSE

Bearing in mind that United States domestic civil rights laws and international human rights laws operate from distinct, although not necessarily mutually exclusive perspectives, this paper provides an initial comparison of the articles comprising the United Nations Convention on the Rights of Persons with Disabilities (CRPD), adopted by the General Assembly on

December 13, 2006, and opened for signature on March 30, 2007, with relevant United States federal laws relating to persons with disabilities.

Current U.S. disability laws run the gamut. The Americans with Disabilities Act, the Individuals with Disabilities Education Act, § 504 of the Rehabilitation Act, and the Fair Housing Act are the most well known. But disability laws can be found sprinkled throughout other statutes as well, such as the Voting Rights Act and Vocational Rehabilitation Act. These laws collectively aim to protect Americans with disabilities from discrimination.

This paper is geared toward understanding the degree to which U.S. law (in form, spirit, and practice) is consistent with the CRPD. Because any comparison is of necessity at times between "apples and oranges," this paper endeavors to analyze the issue in the way a treaty monitoring body would - to see if any area within federal law contravenes the Convention and/or whether there are gaps where legislation or practice might be introduced or reformed to ensure compliance. At this juncture, the CRPD has not been subjected to the scrutiny and interpretation of an international monitoring body. The CRPD creates a Committee tasked with reviewing regular reports of States Parties. It will ultimately be up to that Committee to fill in the gaps and choose between competing interpretations. Having said that, it is possible to set forth a plausible estimate of the CRPD's reach against which to analyze U.S. law.

Synopsis of Analysis

This paper identifies areas in which U.S. law is harmonious to that of the CRPD's requirements, as well as existing gaps in U.S. law when compared to each Article in the CRPD. It also highlights potential areas within the body of U.S. disability laws that would require examination if the U.S. either signed and ratified the CRPD, or desired to have its domestic disability laws and policies be of a level with the Convention's coverage.

This comparative analysis is an extremely important tool if our nation is to consider joining the global community as part of this historic Convention, or simply to reevaluate domestic laws and policies in a manner that would respond to current shortcomings and thereby maintain America's precedence in the field. This paper can therefore serve as background for an informed decision on the issue of signing and ratifying the CRPD, as well as an introspection of currently prevailing laws, policies, and practices more generally. Although the current U.S. administration does not lean towards signing or ratifying the Convention, this may be influenced by a lack of crucial information towards making that decision. Alternatively, future administrations may take a different approach to international treaties generally, and the CRPD specifically.

Several points bear mentioning. The U.S. legal system is a federalist one, meaning that both state and federal constitutions, statutes, and common law impact the rights of persons with disabilities. This paper focuses nearly exclusively on federal law, and specifically on the primary statutes. It is not intended, nor can it be within its mandate, absolutely comprehensive in scope. Thus, while constitutional law and federal statutes rest at the top of the federal disability policy pyramid, there are multiple and various programs within the Executive branch that impact the lives of people with disabilities, although they will vary greatly in terms of longevity, sustainability, and actual impact. The paper discusses these programs to the extent that they have generally been noted by experts in the field to have been sustained and effective.

Explanation of Key Findings

As a general matter, the aims of the CRPD are consistent with U.S. disability law, in respect of which significant segments of the CRPD drew inspiration. For the majority of articles, U.S. law can be viewed as either being of a level with the mandates of the Convention or capable of reaching those levels either through more rigorous implementation and/or additional actions by Congress. In addition to highlighting areas of harmonious thresholds of legal protection, this paper also identifies several CRPD Articles that illustrate gaps between United States disability laws and the Convention. The Articles identified as currently having the most significant gaps between U.S. law and policy and the CRPD are as follows:

Article 5 - Equality and Non-Discrimination. Current U.S. law and policy lacks equality measures such as vocational training, affirmative action, quotas, and job set-asides.

Article 6 - Women with Disabilities. Current U.S. law and policy lacks positive measures sufficient to ensure the full and equal enjoyment of all human rights.

Article 7 - Children with Disabilities. In the main, State rather than U.S. law, governs the rights of children.

Article 8 - Awareness raising. Current U.S. law and policy has no affirmative mandate to alter social stereotypes.

Article 9 – Accessibility. Current under-enforcement of federal laws create a gap between legal requirements and reality.

Article 11 - Situations of risk and humanitarian emergencies. Current U.S. laws and policies prohibiting discrimination in the provision of services relating to emergency services have not been implemented.

Article 12 - Equal recognition before the law. Legal capacity is governed primarily by State-level law.

Article 13 - Access to Justice. U.S. courts have interpreted physical access to court services to be limited by a fundamental alteration defense, and have not sufficiently ensured other access to justice.

Article 16 - Freedom from Exploitation, Violence, and Abuse. Current U.S. law and policy does not provide for proactive education and training to prevent exploitation, violence, and abuse.

Article 18 - Liberty of movement and nationality. Current U.S. immigration policy restricts potential residents and certain visitors with disabilities.

Article 19 - Living independently and being included in the community. Current U.S. law and policy limits the right to live in the community to services that do not cause fundamental alterations.

Article 20 - Personal mobility. Current U.S. law and policy does not recognize a right to the provision of medical and assistive devices in the manner required by the CRPD.

Article 23 - Respect for Home and the Family. State, rather than U.S. law, mainly governs these rights.

Article 24 – Education. Current U.S. law does not seek to develop children's full potential but instead requires an adequate education.

Article 25 - Health. State, rather than U.S. law, mainly governs this right.

Article 27- Work and Employment. Current U.S. law and policy does not provide equality measures, such as vocational training, affirmative action, or job set-asides.

Article 28 - Adequate standard of living and social protection. Current U.S. law does not recognize economic or social protections as rights.

Article 29 - Participation in Political and Public Life. Current U.S. law explicitly protects most of what the CRPD envisions, yet has been laxly implemented in the field of voting rights.

Article 30 - Participation in Cultural Life, Recreation, Leisure, and Sport. Current U.S. law does not recognize cultural, recreational, leisure or sport participation as an affirmative right.

Article 32 - International cooperation. Current U.S. law does not mandate inclusive-development practices abroad.

It is important to emphasize, however, that these gaps are capable of being narrowed or eradicated through either more rigorous implementation of existing U.S. laws and policies, and/or through Congressional action.

CONCLUSION AND RECOMMENDATIONS

The ultimate conclusion of this paper is that there is no legal impediment to U.S. signature and ratification on the basis that, in large measure, the legal standards articulated in the CRPD align with U.S. disability law.

The U.S. disability rights agenda, premised on a social model of disability, has exerted a powerful international influence in revising legal regimes affecting disabled persons. But the U.S. scheme, which is primarily an antidiscrimination one, has limits that are reflected in the gaps discussed above. Specifically, it has proven difficult to transform society's institutional structures and attitudes towards marginalized individuals. Further complicating the U.S. disability antidiscrimination project have been cramped judicial interpretations on threshold definition of disability issues,[1] as well as uneven implementation of existing federal law.[2]

An example of all of these factors involves employment levels for people with disabilities. Observers have alternatively blamed restrictive Supreme Court decisions and noted the abysmal success rates of ADA Title I plaintiffs. Just as importantly, however, are the missing pieces in the U.S. disability policy scheme, including health insurance gaps and lack of training and rehabilitation services, which can actually create disincentives and barriers to work. The overall U.S. disability employment policy has been criticized as non-integrated and lacking in extra-statutory support.[3]

These gaps are capable of being narrowed or eradicated through either more rigorous implementation of existing U.S. laws and policies, and/or through Congressional action. To the extent that this paper identifies gaps or potential inconsistencies between U.S. disability law and the CRPD, the tools of law reform and ratification processes could serve to address and facilitate ratification by the United States.

Signature by the United States of the CRPD would be a realistic aim, insofar as signature implies taking no steps that would undermine the principles of the treaty in question but does not render the treaty legally binding on the United States unless and until ratification is undertaken. Any subsequent ratification process would, as with any human rights convention ratification, entail a careful review of existing law and could be coupled with law reform in targeted areas where appropriate, as well as the use of other tools of ratification, including the attachment of reservations, declarations and understandings that have facilitated U.S. accession to human rights conventions.[4] To provide one illustration, when the U.S. ratified the Convention on the Elimination of All Forms of Racial Discrimination, it attached a reservation in respect of provisions that could have the effect of restricting American constitutional and federal laws according extensive protections on individual freedom of speech. This reservation served to facilitate U.S. ratification of that Convention, and the mechanism of reservations, declarations and understandings would be a tool available to the United States in the case of CRPD ratification.[5]

End Notes

[1] See National Council on Disability, The *Americans with Disabilities Act Policy Brief Series: Righting the ADA, No. 6: Defining "Disability" in a Civil Rights Context: The Courts' Focus on Extent of Limitations as Opposed to Fair Treatment and Equal Opportunity* (Feb. 2003), available at <http://www.ncd.gov/newsroom/publications/2003/extentoflimitations.html >.

[2] See National Council on Disability, *Implementation of the ADA : Challenges, Best Practices, and New Opportunities for Success* (July 2007), available at <http://www.ncd.gov/newsroom/publications/2007/implementation >.

[3] *See infra* discussion of Article 27 (employment).

[4] For a clearly articulated explanation on US policy in respect of the ratification of human rights conventions, see THOMAS BUERGENTHAL, DINAH SHELTON, & DAVID STEWART, INTERNATIONAL HUMAN RIGHTS 359-377 (2002).

[5] See David Stewart, *U.S. Ratification of the Covenant on Civil and Political Rights: The Significance of the Reservations, Understandings and Declarations*, 14 HUM. RTS. L. J. 77 (1993).

Chapter 2

INTRODUCTION

John R. Vaughn

The body of this Paper offers an analysis, by article, of the relationship between the CRPD and relevant sources of United States law. Although these analyses will generally proceed individually by CRPD article and in chronological order, at two points it deviates from this structure. First, the Preamble, Article 1 (Purpose), Article 3 (General Purpose), and Article 4 (General Obligations) are grouped together and compared with the legal framework in the United States affecting person with disabilities. Secondly, this paper groups Articles 33-40, which address monitoring and implementation, together in one discussion.

This Paper also contains a detailed appendix which includes the text of each article of the CRPD followed by a description of corresponding sources of central United States law. This appendix provides additional context to the discussion of the individual articles contained in the main body of the Paper.

PREAMBLE, ARTICLES 1 (PURPOSE), 3 (GENERAL PRINCIPLES), & 4 (GENERAL OBLIGATIONS)

The United States legal framework is directed toward civil and political (or negative) rights protection, and leaves economic, social, and cultural (or positive) rights, when these are provided, to Congress. Thus, concepts from the CRPD (as well as the other human rights treaties referenced and incorporated in the Preamble) such as non-discrimination can be seen as falling readily within the gambit of civil rights protection. By contrast, CRPD notions such as respect, dignity, equal worth, the full enjoyment of all rights, equality of opportunity, mandated legislation and governmental activities, the use of special measures as well as other economic and social rights, and duties relating to proactive alteration of the social understanding of disability, lie beyond the currently conceived parameters of United States law. This basic premise will be developed throughout this paper in the specific context covered by each individual article of the CRPD.

ARTICLE 2 - DEFINITIONS

United States law is on level with the CRPD in requiring the provision of reasonable accommodations, in limiting that provision at a level when the accommodation imposes an undue hardship upon the provider, and in defining as discriminatory the non-provision of a reasonable accommodation.

United States law differs from the CRPD in that the latter does not directly define the term "disability."[1] However, the CRPD acknowledges the social construction of disability in two separate places.[2] Depending upon the ultimate interpretation by the monitoring committee,[3] this definition may ultimately be harmonious with the definition set forth in the ADA and the Rehabilitation Act.

ARTICLE 5 – EQUALITY AND NON-DISCRIMINATION

Current United States law is quite consistent with Article 5 to the extent that it prohibits discrimination and seeks equality through the provision of reasonable accommodations. The U.S. experience with reasonable accommodation was referenced in the UN negotiations on the CRPD. Nevertheless, it should be noted that the reasonable accommodation provision of U.S. disability statutes has not been uncontroversial. There is a documented view amongst some sectors of the public that people with disabilities are getting special treatment or perks.[4]

At the same time, U.S. laws fall short of the CRPD in the extent to which they "take all appropriate steps to ensure that reasonable accommodation is provided" or provide "[s]pecific measures" that "accelerate or achieve de facto equality of persons with disabilities." Thus, programs that are contemplated by the Convention, such as affirmative action, quota regimes, government procurement contracts, or set aside disability-specific professions, are beyond the concept of equality as currently understood in U.S. law and politics. These types of schemes, however, are within Congress's spending power to authorize if it so chooses.

Article 6 – Women with Disabilities

Commentators have noted the problems of intersectionalities of discrimination on the basis of race and sex.[5] Currently, however, federal disability law does not acknowledge this particularly vulnerable population. Any claims for discrimination on the basis of sex and disability must proceed under different statutory theories. Moreover, to the extent that measures as contemplated by the CRPD exceed U.S. concepts of civil rights equality, they are not currently protected or provided for, although with legislative will they could.

Article 7 – Children with Disabilities

Like most areas touching on family law, the status and rights of children are more a province of the states than the federal government. So while there are laws protecting people with disabilities generally, and children with disabilities in the school setting, there are no specific antidiscrimination laws aiming at the protection of children with disabilities more globally. This circumstance is perhaps highlighted by the United States being one of only two countries not to have ratified the Convention on the Rights of the Child.[6]

Article 8 – Awareness Raising

Since deregulation of the broadcasting industry in the 1980s, the federal government no longer requires media providers to act in a socially responsible manner as a condition of licensing. Thus, regulatory mechanisms do not mandate that media outlets broadcast positive imagery of people with disabilities, or to foster attitudinal changes. Moreover, regulation of public service announcements (public awareness raising advertisements produced by a variety of sources, including federal government agencies) which could fulfill some of the mandates set forth in the CRPD, is left to the Advertising (Ad) Council, a non-profit entity that distributes the majority of produced public service announcements. Thus, United States law does not affirmatively require the breakdown of stereotypes through media outlets. Furthermore, one could argue that First Amendment rights relating to freedom of expression protect media outlets from being forced to broadcast particular content.

The Individuals with Disabilities in Education Act (IDEA) requires public schools to make available to all eligible children with disabilities a free appropriate public education in the least restrictive environment appropriate to their individual needs, however it does not affirmatively mandate the breakdown of social stigma relating to children with disabilities.

NCD has evaluated IDEA enforcement over the years and judged it to be a chronic problem area.

Congress, however, could utilize its spending powers to encourage larger social attitudinal changes by providing subsidies or tax incentives to media outlets, or grants to educational facilities, that worked towards breaking down historical stereotypes relating to disability.

ARTICLE 9 - ACCESSIBILITY

United States law covers many of the issues addressed in Article 9, but there are some gaps. The laws discussed below prohibit certain actions and even require some affirmative steps, such as barrier removal. But these laws do not generally force private or public actors to disseminate information or to provide training.

Although Internet websites operated by local, state, or federal governments are required to be accessible under Title II of the ADA and the Rehabilitation Act, the case law has been uneven in applying Title III of the ADA to privately owned and operated websites. In no case has Title III of the ADA been held to extend to stand-alone private websites.

While the laws discussed above have relatively broad coverage and there has been promulgation of standards (e.g., the ADAAG Guidelines for physical places and Access Board for methods of electronic information), there are few current monitoring sources to assess how much progress has been made. Title

III of the ADA, in particular, has been criticized for being chronically underenforced.[7] Moreover, both Title II and Title III obligations are subject to a "fundamental alterations" or "undue burden" defense. Accordingly, although current U.S. law may fall short of that which is envisioned by the CRPD, a more forceful implementation of existing law and/or measures by Congress could readily bring U.S. law on a level with the CRPD.

ARTICLE 10 – RIGHT TO LIFE

United States law is harmonious with the CPRD in so far as it prevents the State from interfering with its attainment.

ARTICLE 11 – SITUATIONS OF RISK AND HUMANITARIAN EMERGENCIES

Hurricanes Katrina and Rita poignantly demonstrated the inadequacy of United States disaster preparedness for meeting the needs of persons with disabilities.[8] Notably, persons with disabilities and their needs were glaringly absent from the National Response Plan issued by the Department of Homeland Security the previous year.[9] Moreover, federal and state agencies failed to incorporate the requirements set forth in an Executive Order[10] and later, recommendations contained in an interagency report[11] before the disasters struck.[12] Bills that would have remedied some of the defects in federal coverage by requiring more effective implementation of disability disaster preparedness policies failed in both the House and Senate.[13] The National Council on Disability has been tasked with evaluating and making recommendations regarding persons with disabilities relative to Homeland Security issues, and so continues to hold public forums on this topic.[14] Hence, both legal protection and actual practice in the United States currently lags behind the mandates contained in the CRPD, although a more forceful implementation of existing law and/or measures by Congress could readily bring U.S. law closer to the CRPD.

Article 12 – Equal Recognition before the Law

Because individual state laws governing the legal capacity of persons with disabilities are assessed on the basis of being rationally related to forwarding a legitimate state purpose, historically Americans with disabilities have been subjected to varying levels of stigma and subordination.[15] Indeed, an extensive catalogue of just such state-sponsored enactments which violated the rights of persons with disabilities was appended to Justice Breyer's dissent in *Univ. of Ala. v. Garrett*.[16] An extreme, but classic and not yet explicitly overruled instance of upholding a state's legitimate interest as against the autonomy and well-being of persons with disabilities is *Buc k v Bell.*[17] In *Buck*, the Supreme Court upheld the right of a state to sterilize "feeble minded" individuals on the ground that it was in the best interest of both the Commonwealth of Virginia and the sterilized individuals "in order to prevent our being swamped with incompetence."[18] Thus, there is reason to be concerned that persons with disabilities in the United States are still not accorded their full rights of legal capacity, although the ADA and Rehabilitation Acts have had the beneficial effect of extending disability antidiscrimination principles to these issues. However, more rigorous enforcement by the federal government, and/or additional programs, could better ensure the implementation of these fundamental rights.

Article 13 – Access to Justice

The combination of the ADA, Rehabilitation Act, and Architectural Barriers Act provide extensive protections in the justice system for people with disabilities. These statutes, however, do not require appropriate training, as does Article 13, although no doubt some covered entities have trained their personnel to create compliance with federal law.[19] It should be noted, however, that access to justice, specifically courthouse accessibility, has often been offered as an example of an area where there is a substantial disconnect between what the law requires and what actually happens.[20] At this point, it is unclear how far *Tennessee v. Lane*, which holds that individuals can sue for damages under Title II of the ADA for inaccessibility in state courts, actually extends. In *Goodman v. Georgia*,[21] the Court declined to address whether *Lane* applied to other types of violations of the criminal justice system. Despite the ADA's prohibition against disabled persons being "excluded from participation in or be[ing] denied the benefits of the services, programs, or activities of a public entity," the Court in *Lane* confined its holding to one individual's right to physical access to courts. In so doing, it left open the question of whether people with disabilities can gain relief when denied access to other state facilities, programs, and services, even those involving the court system; including, for example, the rights of witnesses, jurors, or other participants in the justice system. Moreover, although the reasonable modification requirement of Title II does not include an undue hardship defense or fundamental alterations defense, courts have read them into the statute.[22] Thus, courts determining whether a modification will constitute a fundamental alteration consider whether the change will cause an undue financial or administrative burden on the entity. Therefore, despite broad protective mandates, there are reasons to be concerned about the extent to which individuals with disabilities receive full and meaningful access to justice in practice. Current restrictive interpretations are not inevitable, however, and with more vigorous enforcement and different interpretations of existing law, U.S. law should not necessarily fall short of that which is envisioned by the CRPD.

ARTICLE 14 – LIBERTY AND SECURITY OF THE PERSON

On its face, United States law seems harmonious with that of the CRPD, although both sets of legal directives face challenges in their respective effective implementation.

One element that creates a possibility for a gap in U.S. legal protection is that the provision of services to persons with disabilities under United States law could be circumscribed if it causes a fundamental alteration to a given state's program. By contrast, the CRPD mandates that the "existence of a disability shall in no case justify a deprivation of liberty."

Moreover, as discussed in Article 12, because state laws directly control issues relating to capacity, courts assess whether a statute or practice that disadvantages persons with disabilities is "rationally related" to a legitimate state purpose. In consequence, Americans with disabilities have historically been subjected to varying levels of stigma and subordination. Thus, the protection of liberty and security of persons with disabilities may be vulnerable to judicial perspective. Therefore, while as currently interpreted and enforced, there appears to be a gap between U.S. law and the CRPD, there is no reason why with more vigorous interpretation and/or action by Congress, the two could not be on an equal level.

Article 15 – Freedom from Torture or Cruel, Inhuman, or Degrading Treatment or Punishment

In *Buck v. Bell*,[23] the Supreme Court upheld a Virginia statute requiring compulsory sterilization of people with mental retardation at the age of 18. Although never explicitly overruled, this case should no longer be considered good law. Starting in the 1980's, there was a line of deinstitutionalization cases that culminated in the landmark Supreme Court case of *Youngberg v. Romeo*,[24] which affirmed the Fourteenth Amendment Due Process clause rights of individuals with intellectual disabilities to reasonably safe conditions of confinement, freedom from unreasonable bodily restraints, and such minimally adequate habilitation training as reasonably might be required by those interests.[25] The Civil Rights of Institutionalized Persons Act[26] also empowers the Attorney General of the United States to investigate confinement conditions at state run institutions, including prisons, nursing homes, and institutions for people with psychiatric or developmental disabilities. In the event the Attorney General believes those conditions are "egregious or flagrant," subject individuals to "grievous harm," and are part of a "pattern or practice" of undermining individuals' full enjoyment of their rights, the Attorney General may initiate a civil law suit.[27]

United States law seems therefore to be harmonious with the prohibitions set forth in the CRPD. Ultimately, however, the efficacy of these protections depends upon rigorous implementation.

Article 16 – Freedom from Exploitation, Violence, and Abuse

The primary U.S. response to the problem of exploitation, violence, and abuse against people with disabilities is antidiscrimination law. Its success at doing so, at least in a targeted sense, is certainly an open question. People with disabilities continue to be the targets of harassment on the basis of disability, particularly in their workplaces and schools, in a way that antidiscrimination law has not been interpreted to fully prevent.[28] At the heart of this shortcoming is reliance on negative rights and private enforcement mechanisms. This dynamic, and the consequential result, is at odds with the human rights approach contained in the CRPD. However, proactive measures are within the power of Congress to provide, if it so chooses.

ARTICLE 17 – PROTECTING THE INTEGRITY OF THE PERSON

Current United States law, both statutory and constitutional, formally prevents forced medical treatment or restraint against a patient's will, except in limited circumstances. At the same time, protection of these rights heavily depends upon their enforcement, including the perceptions of judges and other adjudicators regarding the equality of person with disabilities. With the proper enforcement, United States law should be on the level with what the CRPD envisions.

ARTICLE 18 – LIBERTY OF MOVEMENT AND NATIONALITY

On its face, United States law seems generally harmonious with that of the CRPD. And both sets of legal directives face challenges in their respective effective implementation.

One area that seemingly divides the CRPD from U.S. legal protections is that the treaty prohibits denials of nationality and of citizenship on the basis of disability, whereas American immigration policy restricts certain visitors and future residents with disabilities.

For example, immigrants with HIV status have been precluded from entering the United States since 1987,[29] and since 1990 Congressional exclusion of immigrants from receiving public benefits, including health care coverage, have acted as a disincentive to immigrate.[30] Thus, while United States law currently falls short of the rights enumerated in the CRPD, it could be readily amended to reach the CRPD threshold.

ARTICLE 19 – LIVING INDEPENDENTLY AND BEING INCLUDED IN THE COMMUNITY

It must be underscored that the right to live independently and to be included in the community is viewed by many disability rights advocates as central to their lives, and the logical outcome of the protections contained in other CRPD articles; specifically, independent living is often contrasted by those advocates with the type of institutionalization prohibited by the Articles 14-17.[31]

Unlike the CRPD mandate that states "take effective and appropriate measures" to ensure that persons with disabilities live independently and in the community, the right as enunciated in *Olmstead* is not as strong.[32] When determining whether conditions, pursuant to the ADA's limitations cause a fundamental alteration in the provided services, U.S. courts may take into account the economic impact on a state of moving individuals to community-based homes.[33] Specifically, although the reasonable modification requirement of Title II does not include an undue hardship defense, courts have generally read undue hardship into the fundamental alteration defense.

Thus, courts determining whether a modification will constitute a fundamental alteration consider whether the change will cause an undue financial or administrative burden on the entity.

For example, states can consider whether deploying the resources necessary for community-based living for some individuals with cognitive disabilities will deprive other individuals with cognitive disabilities from adequate institutional-based care.[34] This is a lower threshold than that required by the CRPD.[35]

As discussed *supra* in the context of accessibility, and *infra* in the contexts of personal mobility, health, adequate standard of living and social protection, and participation in cultural life, recreation, leisure and sport, the threshold required to ensure that persons with disabilities are not discriminated against in the provision of state provided services (below a fundamental alteration), is likely inferior to that mandated by the CRPD. This, however, does not rest on an inevitable or necessarily uniform interpretation of United States law.

Article 20 – Personal Mobility

Although the United States provides medical benefits to certain persons with disabilities through Medicaid and/or Medicare, these programs are governed through Congressional appropriations. As such, they as not guaranteed as "rights." Further, the extent of the provision of any existing services to persons with disabilities is limited to those which do not cause a fundamental alteration to the individual state programs providing those services. Thus, the extent of how effective measures are, whether assistive devices and services are affordable, the amount (if any) of training, and the autonomous choices left to individuals with disabilities, are all subject to more tightly governed restrictions than are those under the CRPD. Last, positive rights aspects of the CRPD relating to "encouraging" service providers to account for the needs of persons with disabilities lies beyond the purview of rights as currently conceived in United States law. It is within Congress's power, however, to amend United States law to bring it commensurate with the CRPD.

Article 21 – Freedom of Expression and Opinion, and Access to Information

U.S. law is consistent with Article 21. Government at all levels – federal, state, and local – are under an obligation to provide effective communication to people with disabilities, which includes providing information in accessible formats. The federal government has also passed statutes requiring privately owned places of public accommodation to provide accessible forms of communication. Again, it must be noted that this is subject to the fundamental alteration and undue burden defenses, and enforcement of these rights is generally left to individual complainants. There is no reason why, with adequate enforcement, U.S. law could not be on the level with the CRPD.

Article 22 – Respect for Privacy

As discussed above, current United States law does not include disability as a specific "hate crime." Legislation is currently under consideration that would expand the existing hate crimes statute to include crimes motivated by a person's disability, amongst other categories. The ADA protection on confidentiality of medical records is one of the few *per se* violations of the Act. Generally speaking, the applicable United States laws on these issues appear to be administered evenhandedly, although not with any particular protections for disability. Thus, there is no reason why U.S. law can and should not be interpreted to be consistent with the CRPD.

ARTICLE 23 – RESPECT FOR HOME AND THE FAMILY

In practice, States and State courts often appear to rely on stereotypes in determining custody disputes involving parents with mental or physical disabilities, even in cases citing the "best interest of the child" standard.[36] This is an area where although federal law formally requires one thing, the actual practice in state proceedings may not always comply. Moreover, many states do not consider parental termination proceedings to be "programs, services, or activities" for purposes of Title II of the ADA, thereby removing these proceedings from ADA protection and opening the door for disability discrimination based on stereotypes.[37] Therefore, while at present U.S. law may fall short in practice from that envisioned by the CRPD, properly enforced U.S. law could be at the level envisioned by the Convention.

ARTICLE 24 - EDUCATION

United States law has evolved significantly from a time when children with disabilities were generally educated, if at all, in separate specialized institutions.[38] Nevertheless, there are some gaps with what Article 24 sets forth. Current federal law has no definitive provisions facilitating the learning of Braille, facilitating the learning of sign language and the promotion of the linguistic identity of the deaf community, or provisions to employ teachers with disabilities. To the extent that such activities occur, they fall within the province of what states or Congress (through its spending clause powers) may or may not do.

Moreover, in terms of the Article's recognition of the need of the development by persons with disabilities of their talents to their fullest potential, there is a much criticized Supreme Court decision which actually cuts the opposite way. In *Board of Education v. Rowley*,[39] the Supreme Court considered the contours of the requirement of free appropriate public education. The Court held that the IDEA requires educational programming that calculated to provide *some* educational benefit to the child, as opposed to educational services designed to maximize the child's educational potential.

Ultimately, while prevailing, the *Rowley* interpretation is not inevitable. The IDEA is passed pursuant to Congress's spending clause powers, and within these limits Congress has adequate power to appropriate resources to create more robust opportunities for children with disabilities to the level of the CRPD.

ARTICLE 25 - HEALTH

The United States relies primarily on private life and health insurance and medical services, buttressed by the Medicaid and Medicare systems. Although these programs do provide certain services and coverage for some people with disabilities, the main apparatus constraining their application to people with disabilities is antidiscrimination law, such as the ADA or Rehabilitation Act. As discussed above, in some cases this has been successful; in others, not as much.

The existing mosaic of healthcare related disability law has been much criticized for not well serving people with disabilities.[40] The backdrop to this criticism is that "many of the services people with disabilities need for independence and labor force participation – personal assistance and assistive technology being the most obvious – are typically regarded as 'medical' services for which the health insurance system is responsible.[41] The problem is that private insurance often places severe limitations on coverage for disabling conditions.[42] Private insurance policies can exclude coverage for certain named conditions,[43] or impose annual or lifetime caps on permitted reimbursement for specific conditions (even if these caps are way below what is actually required).[44] Moreover, private insurance policies may be particularly inappropriate and ineffective regarding people with disabilities because they trend toward acute, as opposed to chronic care, and typical requirement that covered treatments be "medically necessary," which usually excludes durable medical equipment and assistive technologies.[45] Public insurance, in the form of Medicaid or Medicare, incorporate restrictions that create disincentives for people with disabilities to work. The ability to receive Medicare is contingent on a showing that an individual is unable to do "any substantial gainful work which exists in the national economy."[46] And although Ticket to Work and Work Incentives Improvement Act (TWWIIA),[47] makes it possible for people to work and retain Medicare eligibility for eight years, benefits recipients who reach the end of that period abruptly lose their Medicare eligibility. Although Medicaid varies from state to state, it generally contains similar disincentive rules.[48]

Finally, despite an Executive Order reinforcing the *Olmstead* decision[49] and the Centers for Medicare and Medicaid Services distribution over $120 million in grants in 2001 and 2002 to help states increase community based integration for people with disabilities, states are facing a lack of coordinated community-based services and a shortfall of funds in carrying out the integration mandate. The *Olmstead* mandate is also not unlimited; it considers whether changes will cause an undue financial or administrative burden on the entity.[50]

Although currently U.S. law, as implemented, falls short of what is envisioned by the CRPD, the direction of U.S. law and policy is trending toward the threshold put forth by the CRPD, and that standard could be achieved with proper implementation and/or action by Congress.

ARTICLE 27 – WORK AND EMPLOYMENT

Gerard Quinn has stated that "the mischief that Article 27 is directed towards is the long shadow cast of chronic underemployment of persons with disabilities."[51] The United States approach – which, as it relates to employment, is an antidiscrimination approach – has had mixed success.

Commentators often blame the narrow reading the Supreme Court has given to the ADA, particularly to its definition of disability. In *Sutton v. United Airlines, Inc.*,[52] the Court held that in considering whether an impairment "substantially limits" a major life activity, courts should consider the individual's mitigating measures.[53] In *Toyota Motor Manufacturing, Kentucky, Inc. v. Williams*,[54] the Court held that major life activities are "activities that are of central importance to most people's daily life." The Court has also sanctioned a narrow reading of the "regarded as" prong of the definition of disability,[55] which many had presumed was intended to be a catch-all provision.[56]

Commentators have also noted that the current disability legal and policy scheme, particularly regarding insurance, creates disincentives for people to work, and therefore may be actually working against Title I's goals.[57]

One finding that has been well documented is that most Title I ADA plaintiffs lose. Ruth Colker, for example, has shown that contrary to media perceptions, plaintiffs usually lose Title I cases. Her research shows that defendants prevail in 94% of ADA Title I cases at the trial level and in 87.5% of cases at the courts of appeals.[58] These conclusions are supported by other researchers like the American Bar Association ("ABA"), which compiles ADA Title I results for each year. For 2003, like previous years, the ABA found that plaintiffs lost Title I cases a vast majority of the time.[59] Similarly, Lou Rulli, focusing on Title I cases filed in the Eastern District of Pennsylvania, has found that the success rate is so low that the private bar is hesitant to take these cases.[60]

The biggest gap in coverage between the U.S. disability scheme – which again, from an antidiscrimination perspective is quite strong- and the CRPD involves job training and rehabilitation. Title I was intended as the most expedient method of bringing about social and economic equality for people with disabilities, but additional policy measures supporting Title I have been gradual and uneven.[61] It took nearly a decade, for example, to pass initiatives that allowed disabled persons receiving public assistance to maintain their health care coverage while transitioning to employment.[62]

Consequently, while the ADA forbids employment discrimination the means by which disabled Americans can obtain and keep gainful employment have not been provided. This is evidenced empirically by the fact that post-ADA disabled Americans continue to experience disproportionately high rates of unemployment.[63] The problem is heightened in the most socially marginalized among people with disabilities -- those facing double discrimination (e.g., women and ethnic minorities with disabilities), and the intellectually and psychosocially disabled. Thus, employment-related antidiscrimination prohibitions are only effective when linked with equality measures that alter workplace hierarchies and cultures. These latter type programs are typical of international approaches to disability law and policy, especially within the CRPD, but excluded by the U.S. perspective of civil rights. Therefore, although the current U.S. disability law and policy scheme has fallen short of what is envisioned by the CRPD, there is no reason that a combination of aggressive implementation of existing law, as well as additional steps by Congress, could not approximate the CRPD's more comprehensive scheme.

ARTICLE 28 – ADEQUATE STANDARD OF LIVING AND SOCIAL PROTECTION

Although the United States provides an economic safety net to persons with disabilities living in impoverished circumstances, these social benefits are governed through Congressional appropriations. As such, they as not guaranteed as "rights." Further, the extent of the provision of any existing services to persons with disabilities is limited to those which do not cause a fundamental alteration to state programs providing those services. Last, positive rights aspects of the CRPD relating to an "adequate standard of living" including food, clothing, housing, social protection, poverty alleviation, and family training and support, go beyond what rights are explicitly protected under United States law. While U.S. legal protections therefore fall short of those contained in the CRPD, Congress could affect such outcomes by utilizing its spending power.

ARTICLE 29 – PARTICIPATION IN POLITICAL AND PUBLIC LIFE

With the passage of HAVA, United States law now expressly provides that people with disabilities have the right to vote secretly and independently. Unlike Titles II and III of the ADA, HAVA provides no fundamental alteration or undue burden defense. For some time, United States law has allowed people with disabilities the right to vote with assistance, should they choose. So at least on paper, United States law is quite strong in protecting the voting rights of people with disabilities. It must be noted, however, that this is one area where many policy bodies and commentators have noted the disconnect between law and reality, and so at present the actual voting rights protection in the United States may lag behind that which is envisioned in the CRPD. In the 2000 presidential election (which was pre-HAVA), the Government Accountability Office conducted a survey of accessibility of polling places.[64] This study found that 84% of polling places had one or more features that could present challenges to physical access for voters with disabilities. Impediments included high door thresholds, ramps with steep slopes, and lack of accessible parking, among others. Over a quarter of the counties choosing polling places did not use accessibility as a criterion in making their selection. Social science research demonstrates that the cumulative effect of these problems is decreased voting levels for people with disabilities. The 2000 National Organization on Disability/Harris Survey found that voter registration is lower for people with disabilities than for people without disabilities (62% versus 78%, respectively).[65] United States law does not provide for set-asides or quotas in elected offices for people with disabilities.

ARTICLE 30 - PARTICIPATION IN CULTURAL LIFE, RECREATION, LEISURE, AND SPORT

The United States' approach to participation in cultural life, recreation, leisure, and sport is based almost entirely on an antidiscrimination model. This means that to the extent that such opportunities exist for the general population, the federal government provides a legal right to people with disabilities to participate in such activities without discrimination. In terms of enforcement, the Department of Justice has made accessibility of cultural and recreation facilities a priority.[66] But the larger project envisioned by Article 30, including enabling persons with disabilities to develop and utilize creative and artistic potential, establishing support and recognition of specific cultural and linguistic identities, and encouraging mainstreaming of sporting opportunities, is largely left to private actors and advocacy organizations.[67] Accordingly, a gap exists between U.S. law and CRPD protection, albeit one that could be filled with aggressive implementation and/or additional Congressional action.

ARTICLE 31 – STATISTICS AND DATA COLLECTION

On its face, United States law seems harmonious with that of the CRPD. Both sets of legal directives, however, face challenges in their respective effective implementation.

ARTICLE 32 – INTERNATIONAL COOPERATION

As made abundantly clear in a September 2003 report by the National Council on Disability, the United States has been remiss both in providing technical assistance and disability-inclusive development aid.[68] The extent of State Department technical assistance is itself unclear, as is the accuracy of the disability-related content in the annual human rights reports. More trenchantly, USAID funded development practices cannot be assured of being in sync with the clear mandate for disability-inclusive development practices contained in the CRPD, although efforts have been undertaken. In addition, USAID's policy recommends that foreign USAID missions engage with disability representative organizations in their host countries without providing a framework for those consultations. Finally, the policy does not require USAID foreign missions to consult with disability organizations in order to develop and implement programs.[69]

Given the progressive experience of the United States in developing disability law and policy, it has an opportunity to provide global leadership and guidance (and also cultivate goodwill) by providing greater technical assistance, making development aid disability-inclusive, and mainstreaming disability policies through its own federal agencies, including the Department of State and USAID.

Articles 33-40 (Implementation and Monitoring)

At least in academic quarters, the various enforcement apparatus of the federal statutes discussed above has been criticized as insufficient. The private enforcement provisions of the ADA have been undermined by the Supreme Court's holding in *Buckhannon Board & Care Home, Inc. v. West Virginia Department of Health and Human Resources*,[70] a case that dramatically changed the ways that plaintiffs could recover attorneys' fees in civil rights cases. Rather than qualifying as "prevailing parties" by showing that their lawsuit was a catalyst for voluntary change by the Defendant (the previously accepted "catalyst theory"), the Court held that plaintiffs must achieve a "material alteration of the legal relationship of the parties," such as a favorable judgment on the merits or consent decree.[71]

The public enforcement response has also been criticized as insufficiently responding to statutory violations and creating deterrence.[72] In particular, there has been an underutilization of the class action device and a lack of aggressive use of disparate impact doctrine, particularly in Title I cases.[73] This is despite the fact that public enforcement authorities, including the DOJ and EEOC, have brought such cases in other civil rights contexts. For example, the EEOC moved aggressively – and successfully – after the initial passage of Title VII to eliminate racial discrimination amongst private employers.[74] The EEOC also initially concentrated their efforts on establishing that Title VII prohibited not only purposeful discrimination but also practices with a discriminatory impact.[75] In contrast, despite the fact that the Equal Employment Opportunity Commission promulgated regulations explicitly stating that disparate impact is covered under Title I of the ADA, neither the EEOC nor the DOJ have taken steps to develop the case law in this area.

These criticisms have also been applied to other disability rights laws. Under the Help America Vote Act, despite the fact that the sole enforcement power is with the Department of Justice, they have only brought two cases relating to the disability provisions of HAVA,[76] despite evidence of noncompliance.[77] Similarly, the enforcement of the Fair Housing Act's disability provisions has been criticized.[78]

As set forth throughout this paper, enforcement of existing laws is a key part of implementation. Through improving its enforcement, the U.S. disability legal and policy scheme, while setting forth sweeping antidiscrimination mandates coupled with reasonable accommodation obligations, can come closer to the broad protection envisioned by the CRPD. It is also important to note that if the U.S. was among the first twenty States Parties to ratify the CRPD, it could exert influence on the appointment of experts during the Conference of States Parties. As the analysis below will demonstrate, there are a variety of sources of expertise the U.S. could tap into for this purpose.

The implementation scheme set forth in Articles 33-40 envisions that State Parties shall designate one or more focal points within government for matters relating to the implementation of the Convention (Article 33), as well as submit reports on treaty compliance (Article 35). These precise bodies do not currently exist within the United States government, but it is worthwhile to evaluate which agencies within the current structure have disability-related responsibilities, including an implementation and enforcement role.

The following agencies have a role in implementing and enforcing disability law and policy:

Within the Department of Justice's Civil Rights Division, there is a Disability Rights Section. This is where the bulk of the enforcement power and expertise in non-employment matters resides. The Section's responsibilities under the ADA include litigation under Titles II and III; litigation against public employers under Title I; certification of state and local building codes for equivalency with the requirements of the ADA Standards for Accessible Design; provision of information on ADA rights and responsibilities to businesses and governments covered by the ADA, persons with disabilities, and the general public; and coordination of public outreach activities with other federal agencies with enforcement responsibilities under the ADA; investigation of complaints within certain subject matter areas under Title II including, for example, law enforcement, public safety, courts, and correctional institutions; coordination of the administrative enforcement of Title II by the Department of Justice and seven other designated agencies; and issuance of regulations necessary to implement Title II and Title III of the ADA, including the ADA Standards for Accessible Design. The Section also has responsibility for enforcing the Help America Vote Act's disability-related provisions. The Section also coordinates and ensures consistent and effective enforcement of Section 504 of the Rehabilitation Act of 1973, which prohibits discrimination on the basis of disability in federally assisted and federally conducted programs and activities.

The Housing and Civil Enforcement Section, also within the Civil Rights Division of the Department of Justice, oversees enforcement of the Fair Housing Amendments Act.

The Equal Employment Opportunity Commission is responsible for promulgating regulations to implement Title I of the ADA, and they are also responsible for enforcing the ADA's employment provisions.

Within the Department of Labor, the Office of Disability Employment Policy (ODEP) was authorized by Congress in the Department of Labor's FY 2001 appropriation. ODEP is a sub-cabinet level policy agency in the Department of Labor. The stated mission of the ODEP is to provide "national leadership on disability employment policy by developing and influencing the use of evidence-based disability employment policies and practices, building collaborative partnerships, and delivering authoritative and credible data on employment of people with disabilities."

The Department of Labor is also obligated to help implement ADA Title II and Section 504 of the Rehabilitation Act (including fielding complaints) in areas relating to labor and the work force.

The Department of Transportation is responsible for promulgating regulations pursuant to the transportation provisions of ADA Title II and III.[79] The DOT is also required also obligated to help implement ADA Title II and Section 504 of the Rehabilitation Act (including fielding complaints) in areas relating to transportation, including highways, public transportation, traffic management (non-law enforcement), automobile licensing and inspection, and driver licensing.[80]

The United States Access Board is a federal agency devoted to accessible design. The Board develops and maintains design criteria for the built environment, transit vehicles, telecommunications equipment, and for electronic and information technology. It also provides technical assistance and training on these requirements and on accessible design and continues to enforce accessibility standards that cover federally funded facilities. The Access Board is tasked with developing standards for electronic accessibility under Section 508 and physical accessibility under ADA Title III (the ADAAG guidelines), amongst others.

The Department of Education is responsible for promulgating regulations and enforcing parts of Section 504 of the Rehabilitation Act.[81] It is also obligated to help implement ADA Title II (including fielding complaints) in areas relating to the operation of elementary and secondary education systems and institutions, institutions of higher education and vocational education (other than schools of medicine, dentistry, nursing, and other health-related schools), and libraries.[82]

The Department of Agriculture is required to help implement ADA Title II and Section 504 of the Rehabilitation Act (including fielding complaints) in areas relating to farming and the raising of livestock, including extension services.[83]

The Department of Health and Human Services is required to help implement ADA Title II and Section 504 of the Rehabilitation Act (including fielding complaints) in areas relating to the provision of health care and social services, including schools of medicine, dentistry, nursing, and other health-related schools, the operation of health care and social service providers and institutions, including "grass-roots" and community services organizations and programs, and preschool and daycare programs.[84]

The Department of Housing and Urban Development's responsibilities include implementing and enforcing the Fair Housing Act, Section 504 of the Rehabilitation Act of 1973, and the Architectural Barriers Act of 1968. HUD is also required to help implement ADA Title II (including fielding complaints) in areas relating to state and local public housing, and housing assistance and referral.[85]

The Department of the Interior is required to help implement ADA Title II and Section 504 of the Rehabilitation Act (including fielding complaints) in areas relating to lands and natural resources, including parks and recreation, water and waste management, environmental protection, energy, historic and cultural preservation, and museums.[86]

Finally, although the monitoring and implementation provisions of the CRPD and its Optional Protocol are the product of a different legal regime, it bears noting that several provisions go beyond what is usually conceived in U.S. disability law. The CRPD monitoring body may, for example, elicit the expertise and input of NGOs[87] and UN specialized agencies and organs,[88] conduct proactive inquiries,[89] and conduct Conferences of States Parties to discuss broader implementation strategies.[90] The National Council on Disability currently engages in several of these activities, although not in an adjudicatory capacity.

CONCLUSION

Overall, U.S. disability law and policy can be viewed as harmonious with the CRPD. This is not coincidental, as significant parts of the CRPD drew inspiration from the ADA and other U.S. disability statutes. But gaps exist within both specific legal areas and in their implementation. This is not surprising because, as set forth herein, the CRPD takes a more holistic approach to the inclusion of people with disabilities. Like other human rights treaties, the CRPD sets forth a full spectrum of social, cultural, and economic measures.[91] In this way, the CRPD provides a useful metric for self-examination, and can spur discussions of more effective ways to use existing legal and policy strategies as well as how to formulate new ones.

Although a discussion of the benefits of signing and ratifying the CRPD lies outside the scope of this paper, it bears noting that disability rights advocates assert that formal assumption of the obligations contained in the Convention would establish a clearer mandate for increasing the legal and social protection of people with disabilities, and also ensure more effective monitoring of these mandates. Moreover, if the U.S. was among the first twenty States Parties to ratify, it could exert influence on the appointment of experts during the initial Conference of States Parties.

The gaps between United States law and the CRPD are not insurmountable, and should not stand as an obstacle to U.S. consideration of signing and ratifying this historic Convention. Most gaps can be closed through more aggressive implementation and enforcement of existing laws, combined, in some areas, with additional funding and/or legislative action by Congress. Additional federal measures supporting actions already in place by some states would also move the overall U.S. federal system closer to that envisioned by the CRPD.

End Notes

[1] The same holds true for the European Union's employment discrimination directive. *See* Council of Europe Directive Establishing a Framework for Equal Treatment in Employment and Occupation, 200/78/EC (27 November, 2000).

[2] *See* Preamble paragraph (e) ("*Recognizing* that disability is an evolving concept and that disability results from the interaction between persons with impairments and attitudinal and environmental barriers that hinders their full and effective participation in society on an equal basis with others") (emphasis in original); art. 1 (conceiving that disability results from "interaction with various barriers" that hinder "full and effective participation in society on an equal basis with others.").

[3] *See* Janet E. Lord & Michael Ashley Stein, *The Committee on the Rights of Persons with Disabilities, in* THE UNITED NATIONS AND HUMAN RIGHTS: A CRITICAL APPRAISAL ____ (Philip Alston & Frédéric Mégret eds., 2008).

[4] *See* Cary LaCheen, *Achy Breaky Pelvis, Lumber Lung and Juggler's Despair: The Portrayal of the Americans with Disabilities Act on Television and Radio*, 21 BERKELEY J. EMP. & LAB. L. 223 (2000); see also National Council on Disability, *The Americans with Disabilities Act Policy Brief Series: Righting the ADA – No. 5: Negative Media Portrayals of the ADA* (February, 2003).

[5] *See, e.g.*, Karen Nutter, *Domestic Violence in the Lives of Women with Disabilities: No (Accessible) Shelter from the Storm*, 13 S. CAL. L. & WOMEN'S STUD. 329 (2004); Melissa Cole, *Beyond Sex Discrimination: Why Employers Discriminate When Their Employee Health Plans Exclude Contraceptives From Prescription Coverage*, 43 ARIZ. L. REV. 501 (2001).

[6] G.A. Res. 44/25, U.N. GAOR, 44th Sess., Supp. No. 49, at 161, U.N. Doc. A/44/49 (1989).

[7] *See* Ruth Colker, *ADA Title III: A Fragile Compromise,* 21 BERKELEY J. EMP. & LAB. L. 377 (2000) (suggesting that Title III's broad coverage was a trade-off for weak enforcement mechanisms); *see also* Michael Waterstone, *The Untold Story of the Rest of the Americans with Disabilities Act*, 58 VAND. L. REV. 1807, 1853–74 (2005) (on underenforcement of Title III of ADA); Samuel R. Bagenstos, *The Perversity of Limited Civil Rights Remedies: The Case of "Abusive" ADA Litigation*, 54 U.C.L.A. L. REV. 1 (2006) (same).

[8] A thorough evaluation is set forth in the National Council on Disability's April 2005 report, *Saving Lives: Including People with Disabilities in Emergency Planning, available online at* <http://www.ncd.gov/newsroom/publications/2005/saving_lives.htm >.

[9] U.S. Dep't of Homeland Security, *National Response Plan* iii (2004), *available at* <http://www.dhs.gov/xlibrary/assets/NRPbaseplan.pdf>.

[10] Exec. Order No. 13,347, 69 Fed. Reg. 44,573 (July 22, 2004).

[11] U.S. Dep't of Homeland Security Office for Civil Rights and Civil Liberties, *Individuals with Disabilities in Emergency Preparedness* (2005), *available online at* <http://www.dhs.gov/xlibrary/assets >.

[12] *See* Janet E. Lord, Michael E. Waterstone, & Michael Ashley Stein, *Natural Disasters and People with Disabilities, in* POST DISASTER RECOVERY AND REDEVELOPMENT: HURRICANE KATRINA AND BEYOND ___ (Robin Paul Malloy ed. 2007).

[13] S. 2124, 109th Cong. § 1 (2005); H.R. 4704, 109th Cong. § 2 (2006).

[14] *See, e.g.,* National Council on Disability to Discuss Emergency Preparedness for People with Disabilities at Boston Meeting (NCD News Advisory #07-547; November 20, 2007), *available online at* <http://www.ncd.gov/newsroom/news/2007/a07-547.htm>.

[15] See Anita Silvers & Michael Ashley Stein, *Disability, Equal Protection, and the Supreme Court: Standing at the Crossroads of Progressive and Retrogressive Logic in Constitutional Classification*, 35 U. MICH. J. L. REFORM 81 (2002).

[16] 535 U.S. 356, 376 (2001).

[17] 274 U.S. 200 (1927).

[18] *Id.* at 206-07. *See also* Anita Silvers & Michael Ashley Stein, *Disability and the Social Contract*, 74 U. CHI. L. REV. ___ (2007).

[19] *See* Americans with Disabilities Act Information for Law Enforcement, promulgated by the Department of Justice, *available online at* <http://www.usdoj.gov/crt/ada/policeinfo.html >.

[20] *See* Waterstone, *Untold Story, supra* note 12, at 1857-58 (showing results of California, Texas, New York, Missouri, and Florida studies demonstrating substantial courthouse inaccessibility).

[21] 546 U.S. 151 (2006).

[22] *See, e.g.,*Olmstead v. Zimring, 527 U.S. 581, 597, 603-04 (1999).

[23] 274 U.S. 200 (1927).

[24] 457 U.S. 307 (1982).

[25] *Id.*

[26] 42 U.S.C. §1997 *et seq.*

[27] *Id.* Additional information is posted on the U.S. Department of Justice Civil Rights Division Special Litigation Section website, *available online at* <http://www.usdoj.gov/crt/split/ >. A detailed history of deinstitutionalization can be found at <http://www.mdri.com .>

[28] *See generally* MARK WEBER, DISABILITY HARASSMENT (2007).

[29] *See* Amy L. Fairchild & Eilen A. Tynan, *Policies of Containment: Immigration in the Era of AIDS*, 84 AM. J. PUB. HEALTH 2011 (1994).

[30] See Mark C. Weber, *Opening the Golden Door: Disability and the Law of Immigration*, 8 J. GENDER R.& JUS.162 (2004).

[31] *See generally*, MICHAEL L. PERLIN, ET. AL., INTERNATIONAL HUMAN RIGHTS AND COMPARATIVE MENTAL DISABILITY LAW: CASES & MATERIALS (2006). Practical examples of this type of advocacy are set forth on the website of Mental Disability Rights Advocates, *available online at*: <http://www.mdri.org >.

[32] *See* Silvers & Stein, *Disability and the Social Contract*, *supra* note 23.

[33] Consider, for example, the competing claims facing the court in *Townsend v Quasim*, 328 F3d 511, 520 (9th Cir 2003):

Plaintiffs have asserted that it is cheaper on a per capita basis to provide long-term care services to individuals in a community-based setting rather than a nursing home. . . . At the same time, even if extension of community-based long term care services to the medically needy were to generate greater expenses for the state's Medicaid program, it is unclear whether these extra costs would, in fact, compel cutbacks in services to other Medicaid recipients.

[34] *Olmstead*, 527 US at 597 ("In evaluating a State's fundamental-alteration defense, the District Court must consider . . . not only the cost of providing community-based care to the litigants, but also the range of services the State provides others with mental disabilities."). *See also* Frederick L. v Department of Public Welfare of Pennsylvania, 364 F3d 487, 494–95 (3d Cir 2004) (considering budget constraints and other factors).

[35] Ironically, several commentators make the point that this type of social interaction is key to an understanding of the ADA's definition of major life activity, as well as to effectuating its goals of social inclusion. *See, e.g.,* Ann Hubbard, *The Major Life Activity of Belonging*, 39 WAKE FOREST L.REV.215 (2004); Ann Hubbard, *Meaningful Lives and Major Life Activities*, 55 ALA.L.REV.997 (2004).

[36] *See, e.g.*, Susan Kerr, *The Application of the Americans with Disabilities Act to the Termination of the Parental Rights of Individuals with Mental Disabilities*, 16 J. CONTEMP. HEALTH L. & POL'Y 387 (2000); *see also* In Bednarski v. Bednarski, 366 N.W.2d 69, 73 (Mich. Ct. App. 1985), (reversing the trial court's termination a deaf woman's custody of her "[t]wo normal children," citing her deafness); Clark v. Madden, 725 N.E.2d 100, 103 (Ind. Ct. App. 2000) (reversing trial court's ordering a blind father – a successful CEO of a computer company –to be accompanied at all times by a "responsible adult" while caring for his daughter, simply because of his disability); In re Marriage of R.R., 575 S.W.2d 766, 768 (Mo. Ct. App. 1978) (reversing order of trial judge awarding custody to "immoral" and "dishonest" mother because of unsubstantiated fear that the children would be "emotionally damaged because of [the father's] handicap," multiple sclerosis).

[37] *See, e.g.*, In re C.M., 556 P.2d 514, 515 (Wyo. 1976) (relying on testimony and conclusions of witness who think that people with intellectual disabilities should not act as parents). The Supreme Court recently declined to grant *certiorari* on the issue of whether parental termination proceedings are covered by Title II of the ADA. *See* Irving N. v. Rhode Island Department of Children, Youth, and Families, 127 S.Ct. 1372 (2007).

[38] *See* Daniel H. Melvin II, *The Desegregation of Children with Disabilities*, 44 DEPAUL L. REV. 599, 603 (1995) ("The history of educating children with disabilities in the United States is a tale of neglect and exclusion.").

[39] 458 U.S. 176 (1982).

[40] *See* Samuel R. Bagenstos, *The Future of Disability Law*, 114 YALE L. J. 1 (2005).

[41] *Id.* at 26.

[42] *Id.* at 28-29.

[43] *See* General Accountancy Office, *Private Health Insurance: Millions Relying on Individual Market Face Cost and Coverage Trade Offs* 43 (1996) (listing, among others, asthma, cleft palate, and glaucoma).

[44] *See* National Council on Disability, *Making Health Care Reform Work for Americans with Disabilities: Summary Information on Five "Town Meetings" on Health Care Reform* 9 (1994).

[45] *Id.* at 29-31.

[46] 42 U.S.C. § 423(d)(2)(A).

[47] § 42 U.S.C. § 426(b)

[48] *See* Bagenstos, *The Future of Disability Law, supra* note 45, at 33-34.

[49] Exec. Order No. 13,217, 66 F.R. 33155 (June 18, 2001) ("Community-Based Alternatives for Individuals with Disabilities").

[50] *See* Olmstead, 527 U.S. at 603-04.

[51] GERARD QUINN, THE UN CONVENTION ON THE HUMAN RIGHTS OF PERSONS WITH DISABILITIES 16 (June 10, 2007), *available at* <www.nhri.net/2007/Berlin-Quinn2.pdf>.

[52] 527 U.S. 471 (1999).

[53] *See* Albertson's, Inc. v. Kirkingburg, 527 U.S. 555, 565-66 (1999) (holding that plaintiff may not be protected under the ADA, despite having vision in only one eye, because his brain has developed subconscious adjustments to compensate for reduced depth perception); Murphy v. United Parcel Service, Inc., 527 U.S. 516, 518-19 (1999) (holding that the plaintiff was not protected under the ADA because, when medicated, his high blood pressure did not prevent him from functioning normally).

[54] 534 U.S. 184 (2002)

[55] *See Sutton*, 527 U.S. at 491.

[56] Early on, the Equal Employment Opportunity Commission ("EEOC"), the administrative agency tasked with promulgating regulations under Title I of the ADA, took an expansive view of how the "regarded as" part of the definition should be interpreted: "if an individual can show that an employer or other covered entity made an employment decision because of

a perception of disability based on 'myth, fear or stereotype,' the individual will satisfy the 'regarded as' part of the definition of disability. If the employer cannot articulate a non-discriminatory reason for the employment action, an inference that the employer is acting on the basis of 'myth, fear, or stereotype' can be drawn." 29 C.F.R. pt. 1630, app., § 1630.2(1) (2004).

[57] *See generally* Bagenstos, *The Future of Disability Law, supra* note 45

[58] *See* Ruth Colker, *Winning and Losing Under the ADA*, 62 OHIO ST. L. J. 240 (2001).

[59] *See* Amy L. Allbricht, *ABA Special Feature: 2003 Employment Decisions Under the ADA Title I – Survey Update*, 28 MENTAL & PHYSICAL L. REP. 319 (2003).

[60] *See* Louis S. Rulli & Jason A. Leckerman, *Unfinished Business: The Fading Promise of ADA Enforcement in Federal Courts Under Title I and its Impact Upon the Poor*, 8 J. GENDER, RACE, & JUST. 595 (2005).

[61] *See* Samuel R. Bagenstos, *The Americans with Disabilities Act as Welfare Reform*, 44 WM. & MARY L. REV. 921 (2003) (disability rights advocates sold the ADA to Congress in large measure as a means of increasing employment and thus decreasing public benefit dependence).

[62] Information on the Ticket to Work and Work Incentives Improvement Act and the Workforce Investment Act, is *available online at* <http://disability >.

[63] For example, the Cornell University Rehabilitation and Research Training Center on Disability Demographics and Statistics 2005 DISABILITY STATUS REPORTS indicates that the 2005 employment rate among working age people with disabilities was 38%. *Available online at* <http://www.ilr.cornell.edu/ped/disabilitystatistics/StatusReports/2005-pdf/2005-StatusReports_US.pdf?CFID=13754524&CFTOKEN=34477900 >.

[64] *See* U.S. Gen. Accounting Office, *Report to Congressional Requesters, Voters with Disabilities--Access to Polling Places and Alternative Voting Methods* (Oct. 2001), available at <http:// www.gao.gov/new.items/d02107.pdf >.

[65] *See* 2000 Nat'l Org. on Disability/Harris Survey of Americans with Disabilities 83 (2000).

[66] The Department has participated in several line-of-sight movie theater cases, as discussed above; has made the accessibility of public gathering places an important part of its Project Civic Access settlements, *see* <http://www.ada.gov/civicac.html >; and has taken an active role in the accessibility of sports stadiums. *See* Disability Rights Online News, *available at* <http://www.ada.gov/newsltr1007.html > (highlighting DOJ role in accessibility features of new Washington Nationals baseball stadium). The DOJ has also recently sought to intervene in *Michigan Paralyzed Veterans of America v. University of Michigan*, a lawsuit filed in the Eastern District of Michigan challenging the accessibility of the University of Michigan football stadium for individuals with mobility disabilities.

[67] One such organization is *Sport in Society*, operated out of Northeastern University. *See* http://www.sportinsociety.org/vpd/dis.php.

[68] *See* National Council on Disability, *Foreign Policy and Disability: Legislative Strategies and Civil Rights Protections to Ensure Inclusion of People with Disabilities* 21-22 (September, 2003), *available online at* <http://www.ncd.gov/newsroom/publications/2003/foreign03.htm >.

[69] *Id.*.

[70] 532 U.S. 598 (2001).

[71] *See* Catherine R. Albiston & Laura Beth Nielsen, *The Procedural Attack on Civil Rights: The Empirical Reality of Buckhannon for the Private Attorney General*, 54 UCLA L. REV. 1047 (2007) (arguing that Court decisions have negative effects for private organizations that bring civil rights cases); *see also* Samuel R. Bagenstos, *The Perversity of Limited Civil Rights Remedies: The Case of "Abusive" ADA Litigation*, 54 UCLA L. REV. 1 (2006) (critiquing private enforcement of Title III of the Americans with Disabilities Act).

[72] *See* Waterstone, *supra* note 12 (arguing that Titles II and III of the ADA are underenforced, in large part because of tepid public enforcement); *see also* National Council on Disability, *Promises to Keep: A Decade of Federal Enforcement of the Americans with Disabilities Act*

3 (July, 2000) ("Federal agencies charged with enforcement and policy development under the ADA, to varying degrees, have been overly cautious, reactive, and lacking any coherent and unifying national strategy."), *available at* <http://www.ncd.gov/newsroom/publications/2000/promises_1.htm >.

[73] *See* Michael Stein and Michael Waterstone, *Disability, Disparate Impact, and Class Actions*, 56 DUKE L. J. 761 (2006).

[74] *See* United States v. Hazelwood School Dist., 534 F.2d 805, 812–13 (8th Cir. 1976) (ordering an employer to change employment policies), rev'd on other grounds, 433 U.S. 299 (1977); United States v. Bethlehem Steel, 446 F.2d 652 (2nd Cir. 1971) (ordering an employer to desegregate job assignments); EEOC v. International Union of Elevator Constructors Local 5, 398 F.Supp. 1237, 1264–65 (ordering an employer to develop training programs for minority employees) (E.D. Pa. 1975).

[75] The DOJ was a plaintiff in four cases that all made it to the Court of Appeals level, and established early precedent that neutral practices with a disparate impact violated Title VII. *See* Local 53, Int'l Ass'n Heat and Frost Insulators v. Vogler, 407 F.2d 1047 (5th Cir. 1969); Local 180 United Papermakers v. United States, 416 F.2d 980 (5th Cir. 1969); United States v. Hayes Int'l Corp, 415 F.3d 1038 (5th Cir. 1969); United States v. Sheet Metal Workers International Association, Local Union No. 36, AFL-CIO, 416 F.2d 123 (8th Cir. 1969). This line of cases was a key part of the road to the Supreme Court's decision in *Griggs v. Duke Power Co*, 399 U.S. 296 (1970) holding that facially neutral practices, procedures, or tests that are discriminatory in effect cannot be used to preserve the 'status quo' of employment discrimination.

[76] *See* United States of America v. State of Maine, Civil Action No. 06-86-B-W (D. Maine); *see also* United States of America v. New York State Board of Elections, Case Number 06-CV-0263 (N.D.N.Y.).

[77] *See* Election Protection Hotline Election Incident Reporting System, available at <http://eirs.cs.net.8080/EIRS_WEB/User/logout.do> (110 disability-related calls).

[78] *See* Robert G. Schwemm, *Barriers to Accessible Housing: Enforcement Issues in 'Design and Construction' Cases Under the Fair Housing Act,* 40 U. RICH. L. REV. 753, 768–74 (2006).

[79] *See* 42 U.S.C. § 12164 (Title II); *see also* 42 U.S.C. § 12186(a) (Title III).

[80] *See* 28 C.F.R. § 35.190(b).

[81] *See* 34 C.F.R. Part 104.

[82] *See* 28 C.F.R. § 35.190(b).

[83] *See* 28 C.F.R. § 35.190(b).

[84] *See* 28 C.F.R. § 35.190(b).

[85] *See* 28 C.F.R. § 35.190(b).

[86] *See* 28 C.F.R. § 35.190(b).

[87] *See* CRPD, at art. 4(3). Article 4(3) of the Convention makes consultations with disabled persons and their representative organizations a general obligation and is reinforced by the inclusion of participation as a general principle of the Convention in Article 3. NGO participation is implicitly provided for in the monitoring process, insofar as the Convention requires States Parties to include civil society in the monitoring process at the national level. *Id* at art. 33(3). Moreover, Article 34(3) calls on States Parties to consider consultations with NGOs in the formulation of Committee member nominations as well as in the preparation of reports (Article 35(4)).

[88] *Id.* at art. 38(a) (mandating that UN specialized agencies and other UN organs "shall be entitled to be represented" during the course of considering implementation of Convention provisions "within the scope of their mandate."); *see also id.*(allowing the Committee on the Rights of Persons with Disabilities to "invite specialized agencies and other United Nations organs to submit reports on the implementation of the Convention in areas falling within the scope of their activities.").

[89] *See* Optional Protocol, at art. 6 (providing for a procedure of inquiry to allow the Committee to initiate an inquiry on receipt by the Committee of "reliable information indicating grave or systematic violations by a State Party of rights set forth in the Convention.").

[90] *See* CRPD, at art. 40 (providing that "States Parties shall meet regularly in a Conference of States Parties in order to consider any matter with regard to the implementation of the present Convention.")

[91] Often referred to as "second generation rights," these focus largely on standards of living such as the availability of housing and education. *See, e.g.*, HENRY J. STEINER & PHILIP ALSTON, INTERNATIONAL HUMAN RIGHTS IN CONTEXT: LAW, POLITICS, MORALS 237-67 (2d ed. 2000).

Chapter 3

APPENDIX

This Appendix provides the text of each article (or set of articles) in the CRPD followed by a discussion of the relevant United States law(s) on the topic.

Preamble, Articles 1, 3, & 4 of CRPD and Description of Corresponding United States Law

PREAMBLE

The States Parties to the present Convention,

(a) *Recalling* the principles proclaimed in the Charter of the United Nations which recognize the inherent dignity and worth and the equal and inalienable rights of all members of the human family as the foundation of freedom, justice and peace in the world,

(b) *Recognizing* that the United Nations, in the Universal Declaration of Human Rights and in the International Covenants on Human Rights, has proclaimed and agreed that everyone is entitled to all the rights and freedoms set forth therein, without distinction of any kind,

(c) *Reaffirming* the universality, indivisibility, interdependence and interrelatedness of all human rights and fundamental freedoms and the need for persons with disabilities to be guaranteed their full enjoyment without discrimination,

(d) *Recalling* the International Covenant on Economic, Social and Cultural Rights, the International Covenant on Civil and Political Rights, the International Convention on the Elimination of All Forms of Racial Discrimination, the Convention on the Elimination of All Forms of Discrimination against Women, the Convention against Torture and Other Cruel, Inhuman or Degrading Treatment or Punishment, the Convention on the Rights of the Child, and the International Convention on the Protection of the Rights of All Migrant Workers and Members of Their Families,

(e) *Recognizing* that disability is an evolving concept and that disability results from the interaction between persons with impairments and attitudinal and environmental barriers that hinders their full and effective participation in society on an equal basis with others,

(f) *Recognizing* the importance of the principles and policy guidelines contained in the World Programme of Action concerning Disabled Persons and in the Standard Rules on the Equalization of Opportunities for Persons with Disabilities in influencing the promotion, formulation and evaluation of the policies, plans, programmes and actions at the national, regional and international levels to further equalize opportunities for persons with disabilities,

(g) *Emphasizing* the importance of mainstreaming disability issues as an integral part of relevant strategies of sustainable development,

(h) *Recognizing also* that discrimination against any person on the basis of disability is a violation of the inherent dignity and worth of the human person,

(i) *Recognizing further* the diversity of persons with disabilities,

(j) *Recognizing* the need to promote and protect the human rights of all persons with disabilities, including those who require more intensive support,

(k) *Concerned* that, despite these various instruments and undertakings, persons with disabilities continue to face barriers in their participation as equal members of society and violations of their human rights in all parts of the world,

(l) *Recognizing* the importance of international cooperation for improving the living conditions of persons with disabilities in every country, particularly in developing countries,

(m) *Recognizing* the valued existing and potential contributions made by persons with disabilities to the overall well-being and diversity of their communities, and that the promotion of the full enjoyment by persons with disabilities of their human rights and fundamental freedoms and of full participation by persons with disabilities will result in their enhanced sense of belonging and in significant advances in the human, social and economic development of society and the eradication of poverty,

(n) *Recognizing* the importance for persons with disabilities of their individual autonomy and independence, including the freedom to make their own choices,

(o) *Considering* that persons with disabilities should have the opportunity to be actively involved in decision-making processes about policies and programmes, including those directly concerning them,

(p) *Concerned* about the difficult conditions faced by persons with disabilities who are subject to multiple or aggravated forms of discrimination on the basis of race, colour, sex, language, religion, political or other opinion, national, ethnic, indigenous or social origin, property, birth, age or other status,

(q) *Recognizing* that women and girls with disabilities are often at greater risk, both within and outside the home of violence, injury or abuse, neglect or negligent treatment, maltreatment or exploitation,

(r) *Recognizing* that children with disabilities should have full enjoyment of all human rights and fundamental freedoms on an equal basis with other children, and recalling obligations to that end undertaken by States Parties to the Convention on the Rights of the Child,

(s) *Emphasizing* the need to incorporate a gender perspective in all efforts to promote the full enjoyment of human rights and fundamental freedoms by persons with disabilities,

(t) *Highlighting* the fact that the majority of persons with disabilities live in conditions of poverty, and in this regard recognizing the critical need to address the negative impact of poverty on persons with disabilities,

(u) *Bearing in mind* that conditions of peace and security based on full respect for the purposes and principles contained in the Charter of the United Nations and observance of applicable human rights instruments are indispensable for the full protection of persons with disabilities, in particular during armed conflicts and foreign occupation,

(v) *Recognizing* the importance of accessibility to the physical, social, economic and cultural environment, to health and education and to information and communication, in enabling persons with disabilities to fully enjoy all human rights and fundamental freedoms,

(w) *Realizing* that the individual, having duties to other individuals and to the community to which he or she belongs, is under a responsibility to strive for the promotion and observance of the rights recognized in the International Bill of Human Rights,

(x) *Convinced* that the family is the natural and fundamental group unit of society and is entitled to protection by society and the State, and that persons with disabilities and their family members should receive the necessary protection and assistance to enable families to contribute towards the full and equal enjoyment of the rights of persons with disabilities,

(y) *Convinced* that a comprehensive and integral international convention to promote and protect the rights and dignity of persons with disabilities will make a significant contribution to redressing the profound social disadvantage of persons with disabilities and promote their participation in the civil, political, economic, social and cultural spheres with equal opportunities, in both developing and developed countries, Have agreed as follows:

ARTICLE 1– PURPOSE

The purpose of the present Convention is to promote, protect and ensure the full and equal enjoyment of all human rights and fundamental freedoms by all persons with disabilities, and to promote respect for their inherent dignity.

Persons with disabilities include those who have long-term physical, mental, intellectual or sensory impairments which in interaction with various barriers may hinder their full and effective participation in society on an equal basis with others.

ARTICLE 3 – GENERAL PRINCIPLES

The principles of the present Convention shall be:

(a) Respect for inherent dignity, individual autonomy including the freedom to make one's own choices, and independence of persons;
(b) Non-discrimination;
(c) Full and effective participation and inclusion in society;
(d) Respect for difference and acceptance of persons with disabilities as part of human diversity and humanity;
(e) Equality of opportunity;
(f) Accessibility;
(g) Equality between men and women;
(h) Respect for the evolving capacities of children with disabilities and respect for the right of children with disabilities to preserve their identities.

ARTICLE 4 – GENERAL OBLIGATIONS

1. States Parties undertake to ensure and promote the full realization of all human rights and fundamental freedoms for all persons with disabilities without discrimination of any kind on the basis of disability. To this end, States Parties undertake:
   (a) To adopt all appropriate legislative, administrative and other measures for the implementation of the rights recognized in the present Convention;
   (b) To take all appropriate measures, including legislation, to modify or abolish existing laws, regulations, customs and practices that constitute discrimination against persons with disabilities;
   (c) To take into account the protection and promotion of the human rights of persons with disabilities in all policies and programmes;
   (d) To refrain from engaging in any act or practice that is inconsistent with the present Convention and to ensure that public authorities and institutions act in conformity with the present Convention;
   (e) To take all appropriate measures to eliminate discrimination on the basis of disability by any person, organization or private enterprise;
   (f) To undertake or promote research and development of universally designed goods, services, equipment and facilities, as defined in article 2 of the present Convention, which should require the minimum possible adaptation and the least cost to meet the specific needs of a person with disabilities, to promote their availability and use, and to promote universal design in the development of standards and guidelines;
   (g) To undertake or promote research and development of, and to promote the availability and use of new technologies, including information and communications technologies, mobility aids, devices and assistive technologies, suitable for persons with disabilities, giving priority to technologies at an affordable cost;
   (h) To provide accessible information to persons with disabilities about mobility aids, devices and assistive technologies, including new technologies, as well as other forms of assistance, support services and facilities;
   (i) To promote the training of professionals and staff working with persons with disabilities in the rights recognized in this

Convention so as to better provide the assistance and services guaranteed by those rights.

2. With regard to economic, social and cultural rights, each State Party undertakes to take measures to the maximum of its available resources and, where needed, within the framework of international cooperation, with a view to achieving progressively the full realization of these rights, without prejudice to those obligations contained in the present Convention that are immediately applicable according to international law.
3. In the development and implementation of legislation and policies to implement the present Convention, and in other decision-making processes concerning issues relating to persons with disabilities, States Parties shall closely consult with and actively involve persons with disabilities, including children with disabilities, through their representative organizations.
4. Nothing in the present Convention shall affect any provisions which are more conducive to the realization of the rights of persons with disabilities and which may be contained in the law of a State Party or international law in force for that State. There shall be no restriction upon or derogation from any of the human rights and fundamental freedoms recognized or existing in any State Party to the present Convention pursuant to law, conventions, regulation or custom on the pretext that the present Convention does not recognize such rights or freedoms or that it recognizes them to a lesser extent.
5. The provisions of the present Convention shall extend to all parts of federal states without any limitations or exceptions.

Coverage of United States Law

The Preamble and Articles 1, 3, and 4 set forth the major reasons for the CRPD's adoption, as well as its goals. Below, we set forth the major sources of U.S. disability law, describing both their primary purpose and obligations that they impose. Both these laws and other sources of law (including constitutional and common law) that have some bearing on disability policy will be addressed more thoroughly *infra* in the specific Article sections where they are relevant.

Architectural Barriers Act of 1968

The Architectural Barriers Act,[1] passed in 1968, requires that new facilities built with federal funds be accessible to people with disabilities.

Rehabilitation Act of 1973

The stated purpose of the Rehabilitation Act of 1973,[2] was to "provide a statutory basis for the Rehabilitation Services Administration," an agency charged with carrying out the provisions of the Act, and to authorize various rehabilitation programs. The original primary focus was vocational training and rehabilitation. Currently, the Rehabilitation prohibits discrimination on the basis of disability in programs conducted by Federal agencies, in programs receiving Federal financial assistance, in Federal employment, and in the employment practices of Federal contractors.

Individuals with Disabilities Education Act

The IDEA,[3] (formerly known as the Educational for All Handicapped Children Act of 1975), deals with the educational rights of individuals with disabilitieSpecifically, Congress found that "there are more than eight million handicapped children in the United States today," the educational needs of which were not being met. The Act's purpose was to assure that children with disabilities have available to them a "free appropriate" public education which emphasizes special education and related services devoted to meet their unique needs.

Voting Statutes

The Voting Rights Act of 1965 (as amended in 1982)[4] provides that any voter who requires assistance to vote by reason of blindness or other disability may be given assistance by a person of the voter's choice, other than the voter's employer or agent of that employer or officer or agent of the voter's union. In 1984, Congress passed the Voting Accessibility for the Elderly and Handicapped Act.[5] With this Act, Congress sought to "promote the fundamental right to vote by improving access for handicapped and elderly individuals to registration facilities and polling places for Federal elections." The Voting Accessibility Act provided that the political subdivisions of the state that are responsible for conducting elections must ensure that polling places for federal elections are accessible to voters with disabilities. In October of 2002, the Help America Vote Act,[6] was passed into law with the stated purpose of reforming the United States' voting system. Among other things, this Act provides for accessible voting machines and a secret and independent ballot for voters with disabilities.

Air Carrier Access Act of 1986

The Air Carrier Access Act[7] prohibits discrimination by airline carriers against individuals with disabilities.

Fair Housing Amendments Act of 1988

In 1988, Congress introduced a series of amendments to the Civil Rights Act of 1968, including a prohibition on housing discrimination against people with disabilities. These amendments are known as the Fair Housing Amendments Act of 1988.[8] The stated purpose was to recognize and eliminate housing discrimination against people with disabilities. The Fair Housing Amendments Act makes it unlawful to discriminate in the sale or rental of housing, and the terms and conditions of such a sale or rental, on the basis of disability.

Americans with Disabilities Act

The ADA[9] is the most comprehensive U.S. legal and policy statement on the rights of persons with disabilities. The ADA is divided into three main parts, commonly referred to as "Titles." Title I prohibits discrimination on the basis of disability in employment, Title II prohibits discrimination in the programs, services, and activities of public entities, and Title III prohibits discrimination in privately owned places of public accommodation.

In passing the ADA, Congress explicitly recognized that people with disabilities were a stigmatized and marginalized population that had a history of being discriminated against. More so than in other disability statutes, Congress was explicit as to what it was doing and why it was doing it. Congress found that:

(1) some 43,000,000 Americans have one or more physical or mental disabilities, and this number is increasing as the population as a whole is growing older;
(2) historically, society has tended to isolate and segregate individuals with disabilities, and, despite some improvements, such forms of discrimination against individuals with disabilities continue to be a serious and pervasive social problem;
(3) discrimination against individuals with disabilities persists in such critical areas as employment, housing, public accommodations,

education, transportation, communication, recreation, institutionalization, health services, voting, and access to public services;

(4) unlike individuals who have experienced discrimination on the basis of race, color, sex, national origin, religion, or age, individuals who have experienced discrimination on the basis of disability have often had no legal recourse to redress such discrimination;

(5) individuals with disabilities continually encounter various forms of discrimination, including outright intentional exclusion, the discriminatory effects of architectural, transportation, and communication barriers, overprotective rules and policies, failure to make modifications to existing facilities and practices, exclusionary qualification standards and criteria, segregation, and relegation to lesser services, programs, activities, benefits, jobs, or other opportunities;

(6) census data, national polls, and other studies have documented that people with disabilities, as a group, occupy an inferior status in our society, and are severely disadvantaged socially, vocationally, economically, and educationally;

(7) individuals with disabilities are a discrete and insular minority who have been faced with restrictions and limitations, subjected to a history of purposeful unequal treatment, and relegated to a position of political powerlessness in our society, based on characteristics that are beyond the control of such individuals and resulting from stereotypic assumptions not truly indicative of the individual ability of such individuals to participate in, and contribute to, society;

(8) the Nation's proper goals regarding individuals with disabilities are to assure equality of opportunity, full participation, independent living, and economic self-sufficiency for such individuals; and

(9) the continuing existence of unfair and unnecessary discrimination and prejudice denies people with disabilities the opportunity to compete on an equal basis and to pursue those opportunities for which our free society is justifiably famous, and costs the United States billions of dollars in unnecessary expenses resulting from dependency and nonproductivity.[10]

Congress stated its purpose as:

(1) to provide a clear and comprehensive national mandate for the elimination of discrimination against individuals with disabilities;
(2) to provide clear, strong, consistent, enforceable standards addressing discrimination against individuals with disabilities;
(3) to ensure that the Federal Government plays a central role in enforcing the standards established in this chapter on behalf of individuals with disabilities; and
(4) to invoke the sweep of congressional authority, including the power to enforce the fourteenth amendment and to regulate commerce, in order to address the major areas of discrimination faced day-to-day by people with disabilities.[11]

Article 2 of CRPD and Description of Corresponding United States Law

ARTICLE 2 – DEFINITIONS

For the purposes of the present Convention:

"Communication" includes languages, display of text, Braille, tactile communication, large print, accessible multimedia as well as written, audio, plain-language, human-reader and augmentative and alternative modes, means and formats of communication, including accessible information and communication technology;

"Language" includes spoken and signed languages and other forms of non spoken languages;

"Discrimination on the basis of disability" means any distinction, exclusion or restriction on the basis of disability which has the purpose or effect of impairing or nullifying the recognition, enjoyment or exercise, on an equal basis with others, of all human rights and fundamental freedoms in the political, economic, social, cultural, civil or any other field. It includes all forms of discrimination, including denial of reasonable accommodation;

"Reasonable accommodation" means necessary and appropriate modification and adjustments not imposing a disproportionate or undue burden, where needed in a particular case, to ensure to persons with disabilities the enjoyment or exercise on an equal basis with others of all human rights and fundamental freedoms;

"Universal design" means the design of products, environments, programmes and services to be usable by all people, to the greatest extent possible, without the need for adaptation or specialized design. "Universal design" shall not exclude assistive devices for particular groups of persons with disabilities where this is needed.

Coverage of United States Law

Most of the key statutory definitional concepts in U.S. disability law are spelled out in the ADA.

Although both Title II and Title III of the ADA contain guarantees of effective communication, the term is not defined. The ADA defines auxiliary aides and services as including "(A) qualified interpreters or other effective methods of making aurally delivered materials available to individuals with hearing impairments; (B) qualified readers, taped texts, or other effective methods of making visually delivered materials available to individuals with visual impairments; (C) acquisition or modification of equipment or devices; and (D) other similar services and actions."[12] The regulations provide additional detail.[13]

The term "language" is not defined in the ADA.

Each title of the ADA prohibits discrimination on the basis of disability, although they each do so differently. Title I generally provides that "no covered entity shall discriminate against a *qualified* individual with a disability because of the disability of such individual in regard to job application procedures, the hiring, advancement, or discharge of employees, employee compensation, job training, or discharge of employees, employee compensation, job training, and other terms, conditions, and privileges and employment."[14] A qualified individual with a disability is defined to mean "an individual with a disability who, with or without reasonable accommodation, can perform the essential functions of the employment position that such individual holds or desires. For the purposes of this subchapter, consideration shall be given to the employer's judgment as to what functions of a job are essential, and if an employer has prepared a written description before advertising or interviewing applicants for the job, this description shall be considered evidence of the essential functions of the job."[15] Title II's basic prohibition is that "no qualified individual with a disability shall, by reason of such disability, be excluded from participation in or be denied the benefits of the services, programs, or activities of a public entity."[16] Although the statute does not define "qualified individual with a disability," this has been interpreted to mean substantially the same as in the Title I context; i.e., an individual with a disability who can meet the essential eligibility requirements with or without reasonable accommodation. Title III's basic prohibition on discrimination is that "[n]o individual shall be discriminated against on the basis of disability in the full and equal enjoyment of the goods, services, facilities, privileges, advantages, or accommodations of any place of public accommodation by any person who owns, leases (or leases to), or operates a place of public accommodation."[17]

"Reasonable accommodation" is defined for purposes of Title I of the ADA as including "making existing facilities used by employees readily accessible to and usable by individuals with disabilities; and job restructuring, part-time or modified work schedules, reassignment to a vacant position, acquisition or modification of equipment or devices, appropriate adjustment or modifications of examinations, training materials or policies, the provision of qualified readers or interpreters, and other similar accommodations for individuals with disabilities."[18] Although reasonable accommodation is not defined in Title II, the concept of reasonable modifications for Title II purposes has its roots in the Rehabilitation Act. In *School Board of Nassau County v. Arline*,[19] the Supreme Court stated an "accommodation is not reasonable if it either imposes 'undue financial and administrative burdens' on a grantee, or requires 'a fundamental alteration in the nature of [the] program.'"[20] The Title II regulations offer extensive guidance on the reasonable modification requirement. Consistent with *Southeastern Community College v. Davis*,[21] and other Rehabilitation Act precedent, the regulations provide that reasonable modifications must be made unless the public entity can demonstrate that making the modifications would fundamentally alter the nature of the program, service, or activity.[22] For purposes of Title III, an entity is required to make reasonable modifications in policies, practices, or procedures, when such modifications are necessary to afford such goods, services, facilities, privileges advantages, or accommodations to individuals with disabilities, unless the entity can demonstrate that making such modifications would fundamentally alter the nature of such goods, services, facilities, privileges, advantages, or accommodations.[23]

"Universal design" is not defined in the ADA.

The one definitional issue that United States law contains but Article 2 does not involves the definition of disability. For purposes of the ADA, the term disability means, with respect to an individual, "(A) a physical or mental impairment that substantially limits one or more of the major life activities of such individual; (B) a record of such an impairment; or (C) being regarded as having such an impairment."[24] The Supreme Court has interpreted this definition narrowly.[25]

Article 5 of CRPD and Description of Corresponding United States Law

ARTICLE 5 – EQUALITY AND NON-DISCRIMINATION

1. States Parties recognize that all persons are equal before and under the law and are entitled without any discrimination to the equal protection and equal benefit of the law.
2. States Parties shall prohibit all discrimination on the basis of disability and guarantee to persons with disabilities equal and effective legal protection against discrimination on all grounds.
3. In order to promote equality and eliminate discrimination States Parties shall take all appropriate steps to ensure that reasonable accommodation is provided.
4. Specific measures which are necessary to accelerate or achieve de facto equality of persons with disabilities shall not be considered discrimination under the terms of the present Convention.

Coverage of United States Law

The bedrock equality principle in United States law is in the Equal Protection Clause of the U.S. Constitution, which provides "no state shall . . . deny to any person within its jurisdiction the equal protection of the laws."[26]

Under the Equal Protection Clause a government's drawing lines on the basis of disability is constitutional unless the challenging individual can prove that the disability classification is not rationally related to a legitimate government interest.[27] The Equal Protection Clause only prohibits actions by state actors.

Stronger statements of equality and nondiscrimination can be found in the various federal statutes relating to disability. Title I of the ADA prohibits disability discrimination on the basis of disability in employment; Title II prohibits disability discrimination in programs, services, and activities run by state and local governments (i.e., healthcare, prisons, voting, etc.); and Title III prohibits disability discrimination and in privately owned places of public accommodations (i.e., restaurants, movie theatres, sporting venues, etc). In addition to taking a non-discrimination approach, all titles include reasonable accommodation provisions. The Fair Housing Amendments Act, generally makes it unlawful to discriminate in the sale or rental of housing on the basis of disability. This includes a duty to *allow* reasonable modifications to premises and to *make* reasonable accommodations to rules, policies, practices, or services. The Help America Vote Act requires each polling place to have one voting machine that enables people with disabilities to vote secretly and independently. Section 504 of the Rehabilitation Act prohibits organizations that receive federal funds from discriminating on the basis of disability, and has been interpreted to include a reasonable accommodations provision.

By specifically allowing for and requiring reasonable accommodation, federal statutory law expressly envisions a scheme where affirmative steps by public and private actors to assist individuals with disability are acceptable.[28] Perhaps for this reason, there has been no development of reverse discrimination cases involving claims against people with disabilities (as there has been in the race context).

Article 6 of CRPD and Description of Corresponding United States Law

Article 6 – Women with Disabilities

1. States Parties recognize that women and girls with disabilities are subject to multiple discrimination, and in this regard shall take measures to ensure the full and equal enjoyment by them of all their human rights and fundamental freedoms.
2. States Parties shall take all appropriate measures to ensure the full development, advancement and empowerment of women, for the purpose of guaranteeing them the exercise and enjoyment of the human rights and fundamental freedoms set out in the present Convention.

Coverage of United States Law

There are both constitutional and statutory protections for women in United States law. The Equal Protection Clause of the U.S. Constitution provides that "no state shall . . . deny to any person within its jurisdiction the equal protection of the laws."[29] In the gender context, courts have interpreted this provision to mean that when the government draws lines on the basis of gender, the classification will only be allowed if the government can show that it is substantially related to an important government purpose. This is called intermediate scrutiny.

There are several statutory provisions protecting women from discrimination. Title VII of the Civil Rights Act of 1964 prohibits discrimination in employment on the basis of sex (amongst other things).[30] Sex discrimination that is a bona fide occupational qualification is permissible,[31] whereas there is no similar provision for race. Under this statute, sexual harassment is actionable if the unwelcome sexual advance was "sufficiently severe or pervasive to alter the conditions of the [victim's] employment."[32] Title IX of the Civil Rights Act of 1972[33] provides that no person shall, on the basis of sex, be excluded from participation in, be denied the benefits of, or be subjected to discrimination under any education program or activity receiving federal financial assistance.

There are no federal statutes that specifically address simultaneous discrimination against women with disabilities.

Article 7 of CRPD and Description of Corresponding United States Law

Article 7 – Children with Disabilities

1. States Parties shall take all necessary measures to ensure the full enjoyment by children with disabilities of all human rights and fundamental freedoms on an equal basis with other children.
2. In all actions concerning children with disabilities the best interest of the child shall be a primary consideration.
3. States Parties shall ensure that children with disabilities have the right to express their views freely on all matters affecting them, their views being given due weight in accordance with their age and maturity, on

an equal basis with other children, and to be provided with disability and age-appropriate assistance to realize that right.

Coverage of United States Law

The regulation of children is largely an issue that is left to the states under the guise of family law. So although not technically a federal matter, a recent Supreme Court opinion noted that "a search of current state custody and visitation laws reveals fully 698 separate references to the 'best interest of the child' standard."[34]

Children with disabilities are protected from discrimination on the basis of disability in the provision of programs, services, and activities provided by public entities; and in the enjoyment of privately owned places of public accommodation, under Titles II and III of the ADA, respectively.[35] Similarly, the IDEA provides that children with certain enumerated disabilities must receive a free appropriate legal education, although the Court has held that this does not necessarily mean that they are entitled to achieve their maximum educational potential.[36]

Article 8 of CRPD and Description of Corresponding United States Law

ARTICLE 8 - AWARENESS-RAISING

1. States Parties undertake to adopt immediate, effective and appropriate measures:
   (a) To raise awareness throughout society, including at the family level, regarding persons with disabilities, and to foster respect for the rights and dignity of persons with disabilities;
   (b) To combat stereotypes, prejudices and harmful practices relating to persons with disabilities, including those based on sex and age, in all areas of life;
   (c) To promote awareness of the capabilities and contributions of persons with disabilities.
2. Measures to this end include:

(a) Initiating and maintaining effective public awareness campaigns designed:
   (i) To nurture receptiveness to the rights of persons with disabilities;
   (ii) To promote positive perceptions and greater social awareness towards persons with disabilities;
   (iii) To promote recognition of the skills, merits and abilities of persons with disabilities, and of their contributions to the workplace and the labour market;

(b) Fostering at all levels of the education system, including in all children from an early age, an attitude of respect for the rights of persons with disabilities;

(c) Encouraging all organs of the media to portray persons with disabilities in a manner consistent with the purpose of the present Convention;

(d) Promoting awareness-training programmes regarding persons with disabilities and the rights of persons with disabilities.

Coverage of United States Law

United States law does not affirmatively require the promotion of positive images regarding persons with disabilities, or the active breakdown of stereotypes.

Article 9 of CRPD and Description of Corresponding United States Law

ARTICLE 9 – ACCESSIBILITY

1. To enable persons with disabilities to live independently and participate fully in all aspects of life, States Parties shall take appropriate measures to ensure to persons with disabilities access, on an equal basis with others, to the physical environment, to transportation, to information and communications, including information and communications technologies and systems, and to other facilities and services open or provided to the public, both in urban and in rural areas. These measures, which shall include the

identification and elimination of obstacles and barriers to accessibility, shall apply to, inter alia:

(a) Buildings, roads, transportation and other indoor and outdoor facilities, including schools, housing, medical facilities and workplaces;

(b) Information, communications and other services, including electronic services and emergency services.

2. States Parties shall also take appropriate measures to:

(a) Develop, promulgate and monitor the implementation of minimum standards and guidelines for the accessibility of facilities and services open or provided to the public;

(b) Ensure that private entities that offer facilities and services which are open or provided to the public take into account all aspects of accessibility for persons with disabilities;

(c) Provide training for stakeholders on accessibility issues facing persons with disabilities;

(d) Provide in buildings and other facilities open to the public signage in Braille and in easy to read and understand forms;

(e) Provide forms of live assistance and intermediaries, including guides, readers and professional sign language interpreters, to facilitate accessibility to buildings and other facilities open to the public;

(f) Promote other appropriate forms of assistance and support to persons with disabilities to ensure their access to information;

(g) Promote access for persons with disabilities to new information and communication technologies and systems, including the Internet;

(h) Promote the design, development, production and distribution of accessible information and communications technologies and systems at an early stage, so that these technologies and systems become accessible at minimum cost.

Coverage of United States Law

Accessibility in State and Local Government-Run Places and Programs, Services, and Activities

Title II of the ADA generally provides that no qualified individual with a disability shall, by reason of such disability, be excluded from participation in or be denied the benefits of the services, programs, or activities of a public entity, or be subjected to discrimination by any such entity. "Public entity" has been interpreted to mean state and local governments. Many of the areas specifically addressed by this Article, including access to the physical environment, transportation, information, buildings, roads, schools, medical facilities, and workplaces are operated in the United States by state and local governments, and therefore fall under Title II.[37] Title II creates an obligation for public entities to make reasonable modifications to policies, practices, and procedures; provide people with disabilities the opportunity o the same benefits of public services; administer services, programs, or activates in the most integrated setting appropriate to the needs of qualified individuals with disabilities; make modifications to facilities; make communications modifications, and accommodations in transportations.

Regarding creating physical access to buildings and access to transportation systems – two areas specifically addressed by Article 9 – Title II contains some detailed requirements for public buildings and transportation systems. Physical structures, or "facilities,"[38] that pre-dated the ADA must be readily accessible to and useable by individuals with disabilities, when viewed in their entirety. New facilities and alterations of existing facilities must be designed and constructed in such a manner that the facility or part of the facility (or the alteration) is readily accessible to and usable by individuals with disabilities.[39] Public fixed route transportation systems must purchase buses that are "readily accessible to and usable by individuals who use wheelchairs,"[40] and cannot provide disabled individuals with services that are inferior to those provided to the nondisabled.[41] Demand response systems (such as city-operated taxicabs) must buy or lease only accessible vehicles, and provide a level of service to individuals with disabilities that is equivalent to people without disabilities. Intercity rail lines must provide one accessible car per train, and can only purchase new cars that are accessible.[42]

Title II also governs public (meaning run by state and local governments) communications, including Internet websites that are run by the states.[43]

Accessibility in Federal Government Activities and Entities Receiving Federal Funds

Section 504 of the Rehabilitation Act of 1973 provides that "no otherwise qualified individual with a disability in the United States . . . shall, solely by reason of her or his disability, be excluded from the participation in, be denied the benefits of, or be subjected to discrimination under any program or activity receiving Federal financial assistance or under any program or activity conducted by any Executive agency . . . ." The Rehabilitation Act, which preceded the ADA, in many ways overlaps with Title II of the ADA. It prohibits discrimination on the basis of disability by agencies receiving federal funds, which is a subset of covered Title II entities. But it also extends antidiscrimination coverage to the federal government (which the ADA does not cover). Importantly, Section 508 of the Rehabilitation Act of 1973 requires that federal agencies' electronic and information technology be accessible to people with disabilities. The law applies to all Federal agencies when they develop, procure, maintain, or use electronic and information technology. Under Section 508, agencies must give disabled employees and members of the public access to information that is comparable to the access available to others. The Architectural and Transportation Barriers Compliance Board ("Access Board") is responsible for publishing standards for electronic accessibility.

Accessibility in Privately Owned Places of Public Accommodations

Title III of the ADA[44] generally provides that no individual shall be discriminated against on the basis of disability in the full and equal enjoyment of the goods, services, facilities, privileges, advantages, or accommodations of any place of public accommodation by any person who owns, leases, or operates a place of public accommodation.

Although places of public accommodation are not expressly defined in the statute, most physical locations that are open to the public will qualify. Title III requires the owners and operators of places of public accommodation to make reasonable modifications to policies are procedures to allow people with disabilities access, to the extent that it does not fundamentally alter the nature of the public accommodation.[45] Title III has several other textual provisions that are relevant to Article 9, including prohibitions on denials of participation, participation in unequal benefit, a requirement to provide goods and services in the most integrated setting appropriate, prohibitions on discriminatory eligibility criteria.

Three other noteworthy provisions that overlap with Article 9 involve communications, architectural, and transportation barriers. Title III defines discrimination to include "a failure to take such steps as may be necessary to ensure that no individual with a disability is excluded, denied services, segregated or otherwise treated differently than other individuals because of the absence of auxiliary aids and services, unless the entity can demonstrate that taking such steps would fundamentally alter the nature of the good, service, facility, privilege, advantage, or accommodation being offered or would result in an undue burden."[46] Title III's obligations regarding physical alterations are similar to those in Title II. In facilities existing before January 26, 1993, Title III requires architectural barriers to be removed where such removal is readily achievable, i.e., easily accomplishable and able to be carried out without much difficulty or expense.[47] Alterations to existing buildings must be made "in such a manner that, to the maximum extent feasible, the altered portions of the facility are readily accessible to and usable by individuals with disabilities, including individuals who use wheelchairs."[48] New construction must be "readily accessible to and usable by individuals with disabilities, except where an entity can demonstrate that it is structurally impracticable. . . ."[49] The ADA Accessibility Guidelines (ADAAG) provide general, scoping, and technical standards for new construction which Title III entities must comply with unless they can demonstrate alternative means of access that are at least as accessible as the ADAAG standards.[50] Finally, Title III contains provisions prohibiting discrimination in transportation services operated by private companies.[51] These requirements track the Title II requirements discussed above.

Notably, every court to look at the issue has concluded that privately owned stand-alone Internet websites are not covered by Title III of the ADA.[52] However, websites that have a nexus to an actual physical place of public accommodation may have to be accessible of a program, service, or activity of the place of public accommodation.[53]

Accessibility in Housing

The Fair Housing Amendments Act generally makes it unlawful to discriminate in the sale or rental of housing on the basis of disability. This includes a duty to *allow* reasonable modifications to premises and to *make* reasonable accommodations to rules, policies, practices, or services.[54] FHAA also requires multi-family dwellings built for first occupancy after March 13, 1991 to be designed and constructed with certain accessibility features in mind.[55]

Article 10 of CRPD and Description of Corresponding United States Law

ARTICLE 10 – RIGHT TO LIFE

States Parties reaffirm that every human being has the inherent right to life and shall take all necessary measures to ensure its effective enjoyment by persons with disabilities on an equal basis with others.

Coverage of United States Law

As indicated *infra* in the context of health, the ADA and the Rehabilitation Act ban discriminatory acts by states in the provision of life saving or life sustaining medical care, so long as doing so does not exceed those statutes by causing a fundamental alteration to a state program. Although rejected administratively by the first Bush administration rather than being adjudicated in court,[56] this requirement was key to negating a proposed Oregon statewide health plan that rationed medical treatment on the basis of a priority list that undervalued the treatment of conditions affecting many people with disabilities relative to those without disabilities.[57]

To date, courts have determined the decisions of individuals against state and other private interveners in the context of end-of-life decisions, to mixed results.[58] Parents who elect to withhold life-sustaining treatment from their newborn infants with disabilities,[59] have had their decision-making protected from challenges raised under the Rehabilitation Act.[60] At the same time, while upholding absolute bans on "physician assisted suicide" in Washington and New York,[61] the Supreme Court has likewise prevented federal challenges to Oregon's law which permits persons to elect, within very limited circumstances, to affirmatively end their own terminally ill and pain-filled lives.[62] One of the underlying elements in these decisions, and at the heart of much debate, is whether or not the end-of-life determinations reflect a divergent societal valuation of the lives of persons with disabilities.[63]

Article 11 of CRPD and Description of Corresponding United States Law

ARTICLE 11 – SITUATIONS OF RISK AND HUMANITARIAN EMERGENCIES

States Parties shall take, in accordance with their obligations under international law, including international humanitarian law and international human rights law, all necessary measures to ensure the protection and safety of persons with disabilities in situations of risk, including situations of armed conflict, humanitarian emergencies and the occurrence of natural disasters.

Coverage of United States Law

The ADA, Rehabilitation Act, as well as general Constitutional principles generally prohibit discrimination against persons with disabilities in the provision of government services, here humanitarian relief in the wake of emergencies and natural disasters. The Homeland Security Appropriations bill, H.R. 5441, signed by President Bush on October 4, 2006, provides funding for certain procedural safeguards be in place, for example, the appointment of a Disability Coordinator.[64]

Article 12 of CRPD and Description of Corresponding United States Law

Article 12 – Equal Recognition before the Law

1. States Parties reaffirm that persons with disabilities have the right to recognition everywhere as persons before the law.
2. States Parties shall recognize that persons with disabilities enjoy legal capacity on an equal basis with others in all aspects of life.
3. States Parties shall take appropriate measures to provide access by persons with disabilities to the support they may require in exercising their legal capacity.
4. States Parties shall ensure that all measures that relate to the exercise of legal capacity provide for appropriate and effective safeguards to prevent abuse in accordance with international human rights law. Such safeguards shall ensure that measures relating to the exercise of legal capacity respect the rights, will and preferences of the person, are free of conflict of interest and undue influence, are proportional and tailored to the person's circumstances, apply for the shortest time possible and are subject to regular review by a competent, independent and impartial authority or judicial body. The safeguards shall be proportional to the degree to which such measures affect the person's rights and interests.
5. Subject to the provisions of this article, States Parties shall take all appropriate and effective measures to ensure the equal right of persons with disabilities to own or inherit property, to control their own financial affairs and to have equal access to bank loans, mortgages and other forms of financial credit, and shall ensure that persons with disabilities are not arbitrarily deprived of their property.

Coverage of United States Law

The ADA, Rehabilitation Act, as well as general Constitutional principles generally prohibit discrimination against persons with disabilities in the provision of government services, here legal capacity. Nevertheless, state laws, which vary by jurisdiction, directly control issues relating to capacity, including guardianship, property ownership and control, and the like. If challenged, the validity of state laws restricting the rights of persons with disabilities can be examined under the Equal Protection Clause of the Fourteenth Amendment to the U.S. Constitution, as demonstrated in the

Supreme Court case of *City of Cleburne v. Cleburne Living Center, Inc.*[65] When so doing, courts assess whether the statute or practice that disadvantages persons with disabilities is "rationally related" to a legitimate state purpose.[66]

A strong exception, discussed in Article 29, is voting, where the Help America Vote Act mandates secret and independent voting.

Article 13 of the CRPD and Description of Corresponding United States Law

ARTICLE 13 – ACCESS TO JUSTICE

1. States Parties shall ensure effective access to justice for persons with disabilities on an equal basis with others, including through the provision of procedural and age appropriate accommodations, in order to facilitate their effective role as direct and indirect participants, including as witnesses, in all legal proceedings, including at investigative and other preliminary stages.
2. In order to help ensure effective access to justice for persons with disabilities, States Parties shall promote appropriate training for those working in the field of administration of justice, including police and prison staff.

Coverage of United States Law

There are several sources of U.S. domestic law that address the issues implicated by Article 13.

Access to State and Local Justice Systems

The various apparatus of "justice systems" that are run by state and local governments – including state courts, prisons, police officer behavior, and access to state court systems, whether as a participant or in other capacities – are covered by Title II of the ADA.[67] As such, these entities cannot exclude a qualified individual with a disability from participation or deny the benefits of their programs, services, or activities on the basis of disability. This prevents blanket exclusions,[68] as well as an obligation to make reasonable accommodations and take other affirmative steps to provide access.[69] Apart from the ADA, state policies of not providing interpreters to criminal defendants have been held to violate the U.S. Constitution.[70]

Access to Federal Justice Systems

The Architectural Barriers Act, requires access to facilities designed, built, altered, or leased by federal agencies. This includes federal courthouses. This was the first law passed by Congress to require access to the built environment by people with disabilities. Section 504 of the Rehabilitation Act of 1973, also covers access to programs or activities that receive federal financial assistance, as well as programs or activities of any Executive Agency. The substantive standards adopted for ADA Title II are generally the same as those required under Section 504.

Article 14 of the CRPD and Description of Corresponding United States Law

ARTICLE 14 – LIBERTY AND SECURITY OF THE PERSON

1. States Parties shall ensure that persons with disabilities, on an equal basis with others:
   (a) Enjoy the right to liberty and security of person;
   (b) Are not deprived of their liberty unlawfully or arbitrarily, and that any deprivation of liberty is in conformity with the law, and that the existence of a disability shall in no case justify a deprivation of liberty.
2. States Parties shall ensure that if persons with disabilities are deprived of their liberty through any process, they are, on an equal basis with others, entitled to guarantees in accordance with international human rights law and shall be treated in compliance with the objectives and principles of this Convention, including by provision of reasonable accommodation.

Coverage of United States Law

The landmark Supreme Court case of *Youngberg v. Romeo*,[71] affirmed the Fourteenth Amendment Due Process clause rights of individuals with intellectual disabilities to reasonably safe conditions of confinement, freedom from unreasonable bodily restraints, and such minimally adequate habilitation training as reasonably might be required by those interests.[72]

In addition, the Civil Rights of Institutionalized Persons Act[73] empowers the Attorney General of the United States to investigate confinement conditions at state run institutions, including prisons, nursing homes, and institutions for people with psychiatric or developmental disabilities. In the event the Attorney General believes those conditions are "egregious or flagrant," subject individuals to "grievous harm," and are part of a "pattern or practice" of undermining individuals' full enjoyment of their rights, the Attorney General may initiate a civil law suit.[74]

Both the ADA and the Rehabilitation Act prohibit states from discriminating against persons with disabilities in the provision of services, here procedural safeguards that include reasonable accommodations.

It must also be recalled that, as discussed in Article 12, it is individual state laws that directly control issues relating to capacity, and hence individual liberty.

Article 15 of the CRPD and Description of Corresponding United States Law

Article 15 – Freedom from Torture or Cruel, Inhuman, or Degrading Treatment or Punishment

1. No one shall be subjected to torture or to cruel, inhuman or degrading treatment or punishment. In particular, no one shall be subjected without his or her free consent to medical or scientific experimentation.
2. States Parties shall take all effective legislative, administrative, judicial or other measures to prevent persons with disabilities on an equal basis with others from being subjected to torture or cruel, inhuman or degrading treatment or punishment.

Coverage of United States Law

The Eighth Amendment of the United States Constitution prohibits cruel and unusual punishment. Recently, in *United States v. Georgia,*[75] the Supreme Court had occasion to consider the case of a prisoner in a wheelchair who alleged that, amongst other things, that he was confined for 23-to-24 hours per day in a 12-by-3-foot cell in which he could not turn his wheelchair around, could not use the toilet and shower facilities, and had been forced to sit in his own feces and urine while prison officials refused to assist him in cleaning up the waste. The Court assumed without deciding that this would violate the Eighth Amendment's prohibition on cruel and unusual punishment.

Article 16 of the CRPD and Description of Corresponding United States Law

ARTICLE 16 – FREEDOM FROM EXPLOITATION, VIOLENCE, AND ABUSE

1. States Parties shall take all appropriate legislative, administrative, social, educational and other measures to protect persons with disabilities, both within and outside the home, from all forms of exploitation, violence and abuse, including their gender based aspects.
2. States Parties shall also take all appropriate measures to prevent all forms of exploitation, violence and abuse by ensuring, inter alia, appropriate forms of gender and age sensitive assistance and support for persons with disabilities and their families and caregivers, including through the provision of information and education on how to avoid, recognize and report instances of exploitation, violence and abuse. States Parties shall ensure that protection services are age, gender and disability sensitive.
3. In order to prevent the occurrence of all forms of exploitation, violence and abuse, States Parties shall ensure that all facilities and programmes designed to serve persons with disabilities are effectively monitored by independent authorities.
4. States Parties shall take all appropriate measures to promote the physical, cognitive and psychological recovery, rehabilitation and social reintegration of persons with disabilities who become victims

of any form of exploitation, violence or abuse, including through the provision of protection services. Such recovery and reintegration shall take place in an environment that fosters the health, welfare, self-respect, dignity and autonomy of the person and takes into account gender and age specific needs.

5. States Parties shall put in place effective legislation and policies, including women and child focused legislation and policies, to ensure that instances of exploitation, violence and abuse against persons with disabilities are identified, investigated and, where appropriate, prosecuted.

Coverage of United States Law

The Eighth Amendment of the United States Constitution proscribes against cruel and unusual punishment. And while the criminal law generally prohibits exploitation and violence against citizens, there are no general federal statutes that specifically target violence against people with disabilities. There are, however, some federally supported programs recognizing the needs of people with disabilities who are the victims of violence.[76] Common law principles of bioethics and individual autonomy (including those contained in state level tort law) prohibit any persons, including individuals with disabilities, from being subjected to medical or scientific testing or treatment without their informed consent.

Article 17 of the CRPD and Description of Corresponding United States Law

ARTICLE 17 – PROTECTING THE INTEGRITY OF THE PERSON

Every person with disabilities has a right to respect for his or her physical and mental integrity on an equal basis with others.

Coverage of United States Law

The history of the United States is unfortunate here. In *Buck v. Bell*,[77] the Supreme Court upheld a Virginia statute requiring compulsory sterilization of people with mental retardation at the age of 18. There is also a sad history of deplorable conditions in institutions for people with mental disabilities. One example is the landmark *Wyatt vs. Stickney* lawsuit, which was filed in 1970 on behalf of a committed resident. The plaintiffs in this class action lawsuit argued that the conditions in Alabama's mental health facilities were inhumane, and the patients lacked appropriate individualized care. By 1972 Judge Frank M. Johnson, Jr. handed down rulings that established minimum standards for providing treatment and habilitation in state mental health and mental retardation facilities. Similarly, in 1988, the Hartford Courant, a newspaper in Connecticut, documented the incidence of deaths that occurred during or shortly after psychiatric or developmentally disabled patients were restrained or secluded.

As a result of these and other horrors, Congress passed the Federal Nursing Home Reform Act.[78] Under this statute, Medicare/Medicaid certified nursing homes cannot use physical restraints unless they are needed to treat the resident's medical symptoms. Certified facilities must care for residents in a way that maintains or enhances quality of life, which includes giving residents have the right to make decisions about their care and treatment. Restraints should not be used without the consent of the resident or the legal representative. If restraints are necessary, they must be used in a way that does not cause loss of the ability to bathe, dress, walk, toilet, eat, and communicate. Residents must be released from restraints and exercised at least every two hours. The holding of the Supreme Court in *Youngberg* affirming that the Fourteenth Amendment Due Process clause rights of individuals with intellectual disabilities to reasonably safe conditions of confinement, freedom from unreasonable bodily restraints, and such minimally adequate habilitation training as reasonably might be required by those interests is also relevant here.

And, as discussed in Article 16, standard Common law principles of bioethics and individual autonomy (including those contained in state level tort law) prohibit any persons, including individuals with disabilities, from being subjected to medical or scientific testing or treatment without their informed consent.

Article 18 of the CRPD and Description of Corresponding United States Law

ARTICLE 18 – LIBERTY OF MOVEMENT AND NATIONALITY

1. States Parties shall recognize the rights of persons with disabilities to liberty of movement, to freedom to choose their residence and to a nationality, on an equal basis with others, including by ensuring that persons with disabilities:
   (a) Have the right to acquire and change a nationality and are not deprived of their nationality arbitrarily or on the basis of disability;
   (b) Are not deprived, on the basis of disability, of their ability to obtain, possess and utilize documentation of their nationality or other documentation of identification, or to utilize relevant processes such as immigration proceedings, that may be needed to facilitate exercise of the right to liberty of movement;
   (c) Are free to leave any country, including their own;
   (d) Are not deprived, arbitrarily or on the basis of disability, of the right to enter their own country.
2. Children with disabilities shall be registered immediately after birth and shall have the right from birth to a name, the right to acquire a nationality and, as far as possible, the right to know and be cared for by their parents.

Coverage of United States Law

The United States Constitution protects the nationality of American citizens, as well as their mobility within the country.[79]

Persons with disabilities are protected by the ADA and by the Rehabilitation Act from discrimination in respect to the provision of government services, including equal access to immigration services and attendant documentation.

Article 19 of the CRPD and Description of Corresponding United States Law

ARTICLE 19 – LIVING INDEPENDENTLY AND BEING INCLUDED IN THE COMMUNITY

States Parties to this Convention recognize the equal right of all persons with disabilities to live in the community, with choices equal to others, and shall take effective and appropriate measures to facilitate full enjoyment by persons with disabilities of this right and their full inclusion and participation in the community, including by ensuring that:

(a) Persons with disabilities have the opportunity to choose their place of residence and where and with whom they live on an equal basis with others and are not obliged to live in a particular living arrangement;
(b) Persons with disabilities have access to a range of in-home, residential and other community support services, including personal assistance necessary to support living and inclusion in the community, and to prevent isolation or segregation from the community;
(c) Community services and facilities for the general population are available on an equal basis to persons with disabilities and are responsive to their needs.

Coverage of United States Law

The Supreme Court's 1985 decision in *City of Cleburne v. Cleburne Living Center, Inc.* held that local zoning ordinances restricting the choice and location of persons with disabilities to live in the community had to meet a rational basis test to pass Constitutional muster.[80] When so doing, the Court ruled that "mental retardation" was not a quasi-suspect classification, such that statutes and practices that disadvantage disabled people by treating them differently do not have to meet the standard of substantially furthering an important governmental purpose. Instead, the classification need only be rationally related to a legitimate state purpose.[81]

Subsequently, the Supreme Court's 1999 decision in *Olmstead v L.C.*[82] upheld a claim by institutionalized individuals with "mental disabilities" who asserted that the State of Georgia violated their rights under the ADA by failing to place them into community-based programs for which they were deemed eligible.[83] Further, the Court ruled that disabled persons were entitled to receive treatment in conditions that enable them to reside in "the most integrated setting."[84]

As discussed *supra* in the context of accessibility, and *infra* in the contexts of personal mobility, health, adequate standard of living and social protection, and participation in cultural life, recreation, leisure and sport, persons with disabilities cannot be discriminated against in the provision of state provided services, so long as those programs do not create a fundamental alteration in the nature of those services.

Article 20 of the CRPD and Description of Corresponding United States Law

Article 20 – Personal Mobility

States Parties shall take effective measures to ensure personal mobility with the greatest possible independence for persons with disabilities, including by:

(a) Facilitating the personal mobility of persons with disabilities in the manner and at the time of their choice, and at affordable cost;
(b) Facilitating access by persons with disabilities to quality mobility aids, devices, assistive technologies and forms of live assistance and intermediaries, including by making them available at affordable cost;
(c) Providing training in mobility skills to persons with disabilities and to specialist staff working with persons with disabilities;
(d) Encouraging entities that produce mobility aids, devices and assistive technologies to take into account all aspects of mobility for persons with disabilities.

Coverage of United States Law

As discussed *infra* in the context of health care, persons with disabilities can receive Medicaid and/or Medicare benefits, depending upon their individual eligibility. As part of the benefits they provide, these programs are a major source of funding for personal mobility devices.

Article 21 of the CRPD and Description of Corresponding United States Law

Article 21 – Freedom of Expression and Opinion, and Access to Information

States Parties shall take all appropriate measures to ensure that persons with disabilities can exercise their right to freedom of expression and opinion, including the freedom to seek, receive and impart information and ideas on an equal basis with others and through sign languages, Braille, augmentative and alternative communication, and all other accessible means, modes and formats of communication of their choice, including by:

(a) Providing information intended for the general public to persons with disabilities in accessible formats and technologies appropriate to different kinds of disabilities in a timely manner and without additional cost;

(b) Accepting and facilitating the use of sign languages, Braille, augmentative and alternative communication, and all other accessible means, modes and formats of communication of their choice by persons with disabilities in official interactions;

(c) Urging private entities that provide services to the general public, including through the Internet, to provide information and services in accessible and usable formats for persons with disabilities;

(d) Encouraging the mass media, including providers of information through the Internet, to make their services accessible to persons with disabilities;

(e) Recognizing and promoting the use of sign language.

Coverage of United States Law

Information Accessibility – State and Local Governments

Title II of the ADA requires state and local governments to not exclude a qualified individual with a disability from their programs, services, or activities on the basis of disability. This includes an obligation to "take appropriate steps to ensure that communications with applicants, participants, and members of the public with disabilities are as effective as communications with others."[85]

The Title II regulations provide that auxiliary aids and services be furnished when necessary to afford an individual with a disability an equal opportunity to participate in and enjoy the programs, services, or activities of the public entity.[86] The effective communication obligation is owed to people with hearing, speech, and vision disabilities. In terms of types of auxiliary aids and services, apublic entity is to "give primary consideration to the requests of the individuadisabilities."[87] Auxiliary aids and services for people with hearing impairments include qualified interpreters, notetakers, written materials, amplifiers, captioning, TTYs and others.[88] For people with vision impairments they include qualified readers, taped text, Braille, large print, assistance locating items, and others.[89] For people with speech disabilities they include TTDs, computer terminals, speech synthesizers, communication boards, and others. The regulations provide that a public entity does not need to take any action that it can demonstrate would result in a fundamental alteration or an undue financial and administrative burden.[90] The public entity has the burden of proving undue burden or fundamental alteration, and the decision must be made by the head of the public agency in writing. Generally, provided that the accommodation that is offered is effective, courts have not been swayed by a request for a specific type of accommodation.[91] Finally, under Title II, websites that are run by the state and local governments should be accessible.[92]

Information Accessibility – Federal Government

Section 508 of the Rehabilitation Act of 1973 requires that federal agencies' electronic and information technology be accessible to people with disabilities. The law applies to all Federal agencies when they develop, procure, maintain, or use electronic and information technology. Under Section 508, agencies must give disabled employees and members of the public access to information that is comparable to the access available to others. The Architectural and Transportation Barriers Compliance Board ("Access Board") is responsible for publishing standards for electronic accessibility, which they have done.[93]

Information Accessibility – Private Entities

Title III of the ADA prohibits privately owned places of public accommodation from discriminating on the basis of disability. The statute defines discrimination to include "a failure to take such steps as may be necessary to ensure that no individual with a disability is excluded, denied services, segregated or otherwise treated differently than other individuals because of the absence of auxiliary aids and services, unless the entity can demonstrate that taking such steps would fundamentally alter the nature of the good, service, facility, privilege, advantage, or accommodation being offered or would result in an undue burden."[94] The regulations define "auxiliary aides and services" to include "qualified interpreters, note-takers, computer aided transcription services, written materials, telephone handset amplifiers, assistive listening devices, assistive listening systems, telephones compatible with hearing aids, closed caption decoders, open and closed captioning, telecommunications devices for deaf persons (TDDs), videotext displays . . . qualified readers, taped texts, audio recordings, Brailled materials, [and] large print materials."[95]

Regarding the Internet, thus far courts have concluded that privately owned stand-alone Internet websites are not covered by Title III of the ADA. However, websites that have a nexus to an actual physical place of public accommodation may have to be accessible of a program, service, or activity of the place of public accommodation.[96]

Title IV of the ADA and its implementing regulations[97] address telephone and television access for people with hearing and speech disabilities. They require common carriers (telephone companies) to establish interstate and intrastate telecommunications relay services (TRS) 24 hours a day, 7 days a week. TRS enables callers with hearing and speech disabilities who use telecommunications devices for the deaf (TDDs) and callers who use voice telephones to communicate with each other through a third party communications assistant. The Federal Communications Commission (FCC) has set minimum standards for TRS services. Title IV also requires closed captioning of Federally funded public service announcements.

Pursuant to the Telecommunications Act of 1996,[98] the FCC has adopted rules requiring closed captioning of most, though not all, television programming.

Finally, the Assistive Technology Act of 1998[99] provides federal support for research and promotion of assistive technology.

Article 22 of the CRPD and Description of Corresponding United States Law

ARTICLE 22 – RESPECT FOR PRIVACY

1. No person with disabilities, regardless of place of residence or living arrangements, shall be subjected to arbitrary or unlawful interference with his or her privacy, family, home or correspondence or other types of communication or to unlawful attacks on his or her honour and reputation. Persons with disabilities have the right to the protection of the law against such interference or attacks.
2. States Parties shall protect the privacy of personal, health and rehabilitation information of persons with disabilities on an equal basis with others.

Coverage of United States Law

Defamation law, which protects against attacks on honor or reputation, is largely a creation of state law. That said, at least one commentator has recently pointed out the prevalence of harassment on the basis of disability in both the educational and employment contexts, as well as the insufficient existing legal responses under both the ADA and IDEA.[100]

Federal prosecution is permitted of a person who "by force or threat of force willfully injures, intimidates, or interferes with . . . any person because of his race, color, religion or national origin and because he is or has been" attempting to engage in one of six types of federally protected activities (including voting or going to school).[101] Disability is not one of the protected categories. Current statistics gathered by the FBI and Department of Justice show that roughly 1% of the hate crimes committed are done so with disability animus as a motivating factor.[102]

There is one place where the right to privacy of one's disability-related medical information is explicitly and forcefully protected. If an employer administers any type of medical test or inquiry, the employer must treat the results as confidential medical records. The ADA tightly controls how this information can be used, and who has access to the information.[103]

Article 23 of the CRPD and Description of Corresponding United States Law

ARTICLE 23 – RESPECT FOR HOME AND THE FAMILY

1. States Parties shall take effective and appropriate measures to eliminate discrimination against persons with disabilities in all matters relating to marriage, family, parenthood and relationships, on an equal basis with others, so as to ensure that:
   (a) The right of all persons with disabilities who are of marriageable age to marry and to found a family on the basis of free and full consent of the intending spouses is recognized;
   (b) The rights of persons with disabilities to decide freely and responsibly on the number and spacing of their children and to have access to age-appropriate information, reproductive and family planning education are recognised, and the means necessary to enable them to exercise these rights and the equal opportunity to retain their fertility are provided;
   (c) Persons with disabilities, including children, shall retain their fertility on an equal basis with others.
2. States Parties shall ensure the rights and responsibilities of persons with disabilities, with regard to guardianship, wardship, trusteeship and adoption of children, or similar institutions where these concepts exist in national legislation; in all cases the interests of the children shall be paramount. States Parties shall render appropriate assistance to persons with disabilities in the performance of their child-rearing responsibilities.
3. States Parties shall ensure that children with disabilities have equal rights with respect to family life. With a view to realising these rights,

and to prevent concealment, abandonment, neglect and segregation of children with disabilities, States Parties shall undertake to provide early and comprehensive information, services and support to children with disabilities and their families.

4. States Parties shall ensure that a child shall not be separated from his or her parents against their will, except when competent authorities subject to judicial review determine, in accordance with applicable law and procedures, that such separation is necessary for the best interests of the child. In no case shall a child be separated from parents on the basis of a disability of either the child or one or both of the parents.
5. States Parties shall undertake that where the immediate family is unable to care for a child with disabilities, to take every effort to provide alternative care within the wider family, and failing that, within the community in a family setting.

Coverage of United States Law

Family law is generally an area that is left to the states, subject to limitations set by the U.S. Constitution or federal statutes. The Supreme Court has recognized the importance of marriage and procreation as among "the basic civil rights of man."[104] Although the Court has never expressly done so, commentators have suggested that this and similar cases extend the basic right to marry and procreation to people with mental disabilities. Compulsory sterilization for people with mental retardation was upheld in *Buck v. Bell*,[105] and although this case has never formally overruled, it is doubtful that it can still be considered good law.

Based on the fundamental right of the nature to keep one's family together, the Court has held that a state can only terminate parental rights through an individualized inquiry rather than a presumption based on an ascribed status.[106]

Some courts have held that state termination proceedings, like all state court proceedings, are covered by Title II of the ADA.[107] Therefore the courts, the Department of Health and Human Services (HHS) and child protective services must make reasonable modifications to their rules, policies, and practices of the services they provide in accommodating persons with disabilities that utilize their services. The services provided by these entities include individual assessments and reunification programs designed to evaluate and assist persons in developing their parenting skills when their children are removed from their custody.[108] Other courts, however, have refused to permit parents with disabilities to assert, as grounds opposing termination of their parental rights, that termination would violate their rights under the ADA.[109]

Article 24 of the CRPD and Description of Corresponding United States Law

ARTICLE 24 – EDUCATION

1. States Parties recognize the right of persons with disabilities to education. With a view to realizing this right without discrimination and on the basis of equal opportunity, States Parties shall ensure an inclusive, education system at all levels, and life-long learning, directed to:
   (a) The full development of the human potential and sense of dignity and self worth, and the strengthening of respect for human rights, fundamental freedoms and human diversity;
   (b) The development by persons with disabilities of their personality, talents and creativity, as well as their mental and physical abilities, to their fullest potential;
   (c) Enabling persons with disabilities to participate effectively in a free society.
2. In realizing this right, States Parties shall ensure:
   (a) That persons with disabilities are not excluded from the general education system on the basis of disability, and that children with disabilities are not excluded from free and compulsory primary and secondary education on the basis of disability;
   (b) That persons with disabilities can access an inclusive, quality, free primary and secondary education on an equal basis with others in the communities in which they live;
   (c) Reasonable accommodation of the individual's requirements;
   (d) That persons with disabilities receive the support required, within the general education system, to facilitate their effective education;

(e) That effective individualized support measures are provided in environments that maximize academic and social development, consistent with the goal of full inclusion.

3. States Parties shall enable persons with disabilities to learn life and social development skills to facilitate their full and equal participation in education and as members of the community. To this end, States Parties shall take appropriate measures, including:
   (a) Facilitating the learning of Braille, alternative script, augmentative and alternative modes, means and formats of communication, orientation and mobility skills, and facilitating peer support and mentoring;
   (b) Facilitating the learning of sign language and the promotion of the linguistic identity of the deaf community;
   (c) Ensuring that the education of persons, and in particular children, who are blind, deaf and deafblind, is delivered in the most appropriate languages and modes and means of communication for the individual, and in environments which maximize academic and social development.
4. In order to help ensure the realization of this right, States Parties shall take appropriate measures to employ teachers, including those with disabilities, who are qualified in sign language and Braille, and to train professionals and staff who work at all levels of education. Such training shall incorporate disability awareness and the use of appropriate augmentative and alternative modes, means and formats of communication, educational techniques and materials to support persons with disabilities.
5. States Parties shall ensure that persons with disabilities are able to access general tertiary education, vocational training, adult education and lifelong learning without discrimination and on an equal basis with others. To this end, States Parties shall ensure that reasonable accommodation is provided to persons with disabilities.

Coverage of United States Law

The primary statutory vehicle for the educational rights of persons with disabilities is the Individuals with Disabilities Education Act (IDEA). The primary stated purposes of the IDEA are:

> (1)(A) to ensure that all children with disabilities have available to them a free appropriate public education that emphasizes special education and related services designed to meet their unique needs and prepare them for employment and independent living;
>
> (B) to ensure that the rights of children with disabilities and parents of such children are protected; and
>
> (C) to assist States, localities, educational service agencies, and Federal agencies to provide for the education of all children with disabilities;[110]

The IDEA provides federal funding to states to support special education services in public elementary and secondary schools. This funding is based on the number of children in the state receiving special education services multiplied by the average per-pupil cost of public education in the United States. The IDEA authorizes federal funding grants of only 40% of that average cost. Congress has not allocated sufficient funds to cover its entire 40% portion of special education costs, leaving states to fund much of their own compliance with their obligations under the IDEA.

The primary requirements of the IDEA are Free Appropriate Public Education (FAPE), Least Restrictive Environment, and Procedural Due Process, and "Child Find." The IDEA requires each state to provide "[a] free appropriate public education . . . to all children with disabilities residing in the State between the ages of 3 and 21, inclusive, including children with disabilities who have been suspended or expelled from school."[111] This requirement is commonly referred to as FAPE. In order to ensure that FAPE is being provided to every eligible child, the IDEA requires states to identify, locate, and evaluate "[a]ll children with disabilities residing in the State, including children with disabilities attending private schools, regardless of the severity of their disabilities, and who are in need of special education and related services." ("Child Find").[112]

The IDEA requires that public education for children with disabilities be provided in the least restrictive environment appropriate to them, meaning, that "children with disabilities . . . are educated with children who are not disabled, and special classes, separate schooling, or other removal of children with disabilities from the regular educational environment occurs only when the nature or severity of the disability of a child is such that education in regular classes with the use of supplementary aids and services cannot be achieved satisfactorily."[113]

The procedural due process requirements of the IDEA include the requirement to evaluate children to determine their eligibility for special education services, provide individualized education programs (IEPs) developed by IEP teams, ensure parental notice, consent, and access to records, and offer mediation and access to impartial hearings to resolve disputes. In addition, the IDEA imposes a "stay put" requirement preventing schools from expelling or suspending students with disabilities or otherwise changing their educational placements without meeting due process requirements.[114]

Unlike the ADA and Rehabilitation Act, which cover any qualified individual with a mental or physical impairment that substantially limits a major life activity, the IDEA protects "children with disabilities" ages three through twenty-one,[115] defined as those

> (i) with mental retardation, hearing impairments (including deafness), speech or language impairments, visual impairments (including blindness), serious emotional disturbance (hereinafter referred to as "emotional disturbance"), orthopedic impairments, autism, traumatic brain injury, other health impairments, or specific learning disabilities; and
>
> (ii) who, by reason thereof, needs special education and related services.
>
> Id. § 1401(3)(A).

For children ages 3 through 9, states have discretion to cover children with other impairments, such as developmental delay, who need special education and related services as a result of those impairments.[116] In order to be eligible for special education, a child must both have one of the 10 categories of disabilities and "by reason thereof" need special education and related services.

The IDEA is not the sole source of states' special educational obligations. There are constitutional requirements as well. In *Pennsylvania Ass'n for Retarded Children v. Pennsylvania*,[117] the court approved a consent decree finding that, under the Equal Protection Clause of the United States Constitution, having undertaken to provide free public education, Pennsylvania must educate all children, including those with disabilities. Moreover, "[i]t is the Commonwealth's obligation to place each mentally retarded child in a free, public program of education and training appropriate to the child's capacity."[118] The court also applied the principle from *Brown v. Board of Education of Topeka*,[119] that separate education is inherently unequal and, therefore, applied a presumption that "placement in a regular public school class is preferable to placement in a special public school class and placement in a special public school class is preferable to placement in any other type of program of education and training."[120] Similarly, in *Mills v.*

Board of Education of District of Columbia,[121] the court granted summary judgment to a class of children with disabilities, finding that the Equal Protection Clause required inclusion of children with disabilities in public education and, further, that the additional cost of such education was not a defense.

Both the ADA and Section 504 of the Rehabilitation Act also have applicability to the education of people with disabilities. Private educational institutions at all levels fall within the definition of Title III of the ADA, and public educational institutions fall within Title II. Any educational institution that receives federal funds – which includes most public schools and universities – are also covered under the Rehabilitation Act. Therefore, generally speaking, these entities cannot discriminate on the basis of disability. Courts have interpreted this to apply to the physical accessibility of campuses,[122] and a requirement to provide interpreters at no cost to students,[123] amongst others.

Article 25 of the CRPD and Description of Corresponding United States Law

ARTICLE 25 – HEALTH

States Parties recognize that persons with disabilities have the right to the enjoyment of the highest attainable standard of health without discrimination on the basis of disability. States Parties shall take all appropriate measures to ensure access for persons with disabilities to health services that are gender sensitive, including health-related rehabilitation. In particular, States Parties shall:

(a) Provide persons with disabilities with the same range, quality and standard of free or affordable health care and programmes as provided other persons, including in the area of sexual and reproductive health and population-based public health programmes;
(b) Provide those health services needed by persons with disabilities specifically because of their disabilities, including early identification and intervention as appropriate, and services designed to minimize and prevent further disabilities, including among children and the elderly;

(c) Provide these health services as close as possible to people's own communities, including in rural areas;
(d) Require health professionals to provide care of the same quality to persons with disabilities as to others, including on the basis of free and informed consent by, inter alia, raising awareness of the human rights, dignity, autonomy and needs of persons with disabilities through training and the promulgation of ethical standards for public and private health care;
(e) Prohibit discrimination against persons with disabilities in the provision of health insurance, and life insurance where such insurance is permitted by national law, which shall be provided in a fair and reasonable manner;
(f) Prevent discriminatory denial of health care or health services or food and fluids on the basis of disability.

Coverage of United States Law

The United States has no universal health coverage system. The closest programs offered by the federal and state governments are Medicare and Medicaid. Medicare is a health insurance program administered by the federal government. To receive Medicare, a working-age individual with a disability must first become eligible for Social Security Disability Insurance by showing that he or she is unable to do any "substantial gainful work which exists in the national economy."[124] There is then a two-year waiting period to receive Medicare. Part A of Medicare covers hospital insurance (including stays in a skilled nursing facility), Part B covers medical insurance, Part C gives beneficiaries the option of receiving Medicare benefits through private health insurance plans, and Part D offers a prescription drug benefit. Medicaid is a federal-state cooperative program that provides medical benefits of different types to various needy populations. States do not have to participate in Medicaid, but all have. States have flexibility in deciding what populations they have to cover and what benefits they will provide, although the Medicaid statute does set have several requirements in terms of coverage and services. In most states, an individual who meets the Social Security Act's definition of disability can receive Medicaid coverage.

To the extent that health care services are provided by private entities, they are covered by Title III of the ADA; to the extent that they are provided by public entities, they are covered by Title II and Section 504 of the

Rehabilitation Act. There is a line of cases suggesting that health care providers cannot discriminate on the basis of disability.[125] Other cases, however, have held that actions which are "neutral" but have the effect of impacting people with disabilities more harshly than the general population are acceptable under these statutes.[126]

Insurance also occupies an uncertain place under the ADA. The courts are split on whether insurance policies are covered as public accommodations under the statute.[127] The ADA itself has a "safe harbor" provision regarding insurance.[128] At least one Circuit Court has construed this provision to mean that the ADA does generally apply to the content of insurance policies.[129] Most circuits, however, have not applied the provisions of Title III to the substance of insurance policies.[130]

Regarding medical treatment in the community, both the ADA and its regulations provide that public entities must administer services, programs, or activities in the most integrated setting appropriate to the needs of qualified individuals with disabilities. In *Olmstead v. Zimring*,[131] two women with mental retardation and psychiatric conditions brought suit under Title II, claiming that the state of Georgia had discriminated against them by keeping them in institutionalized settings instead of community placements that were more appropriate for their needs. The State's professionals had determined that community-based settings would be more appropriate for the women, but none were available. The Court held that this unjustified institutional isolation constituted discrimination within the meaning of Title II. However, the Court recognized that the duty to accommodate was not absolute. In deciding whether this accommodation would fundamentally alter the state's mental health treatment program, the proper inquiry was not the cost of accommodating these two plaintiffs weighted against the states' overall mental health budget.

Article 27 of the CRPD and Description of Corresponding United States Law

ARTICLE 27 – WORK AND EMPLOYMENT

1. States Parties recognize the right of persons with disabilities to work, on an equal basis with others; this includes the right to the opportunity to gain a living by work freely chosen or accepted in a labour market

and work environment that is open, inclusive and accessible to persons with disabilities. States Parties shall safeguard and promote the realization of the right to work, including for those who acquire a disability during the course of employment, by taking appropriate steps, including through legislation, to, inter alia:

(a) Prohibit discrimination on the basis of disability with regard to all matters concerning all forms of employment, including conditions of recruitment, hiring and employment, continuance of employment, career advancement, and safe and healthy working conditions;
(b) Protect the rights of persons with disabilities, on an equal basis with others, to just and favourable conditions of work, including equal opportunities and equal remuneration for work of equal value, safe and healthy working conditions, including protection from harassment, and the redressing of grievances;
(c) Ensure that persons with disabilities are able to exercise their labour and trade union rights on an equal basis with others;
(d) Enable persons with disabilities to have effective access to general technical and vocational guidance programmes, placement services and vocational and continuing training;
(e) Promote employment opportunities and career advancement for persons with disabilities in the labour market, as well as assistance in finding, obtaining and maintaining and returning to employment;
(f) Promote opportunities for self-employment, entrepreneurship, the development of cooperatives and starting one's own business;
(g) Employ persons with disabilities in the public sector;
(h) Promote the employment of persons with disabilities in the private sector through appropriate policies and measures, which may include affirmative action programmes, incentives and other measures;
(i) Ensure that reasonable accommodation is provided to persons with disabilities in the workplace;
(j) Promote the acquisition by persons with disabilities of work experience in the open labour market;
(k) Promote vocational and professional rehabilitation, job retention and return-to-work programmes for persons with disabilities.

2. States Parties shall ensure that persons with disabilities are not held in slavery or in servitude, and are protected, on an equal basis with others, from forced or compulsory labour.

Coverage of United States Law

The United States has several sources of law that bear upon the employment of people with disabilities. As a starting place, the Due Process and Equal Protection Clauses of the United States Constitution, which only apply to state action, offer little in the way of protection for the rights of people with disabilities. As for the Due Process Clause, the Supreme Court held "the right to hold specific private employment and to follow a chosen profession free from unreasonable governmental interference comes within the 'liberty' and 'property' concepts of the Fifth Amendment."[132] But states are free to regulate employment, and the courts will only review those regulations using rational basis review.[133] Similarly, the Court has held that under the Equal Protection Clause, state regulation that draws lines on the basis of disability will only be reviewed under the rational basis standard.[134]

Statutory protection is far stronger. Title I of the ADA provide that "no covered entity shall discriminate against a qualified individual with a disability because of the disability of such individual in regard to job application procedures, the hiring, advancement, or discharge of employees, employee compensation, job training, and other terms, conditions, and privileges of employment."[135] A "covered entity" is defined as an employer with 15 or more employees.[136] Discrimination is defined as, amongst other things, "not making reasonable accommodations to the known physical or mental limitations of an otherwise qualified individual with a disability who is an applicant or employee, unless such covered entity can demonstrate that the accommodation would impose an undue hardship on the operation of the business of such covered entity; or . . . denying employment opportunities to a job applicant or employee who is an otherwise qualified individual with a disability, if such denial is based on the need of such covered entity to make reasonable accommodation to the physical or mental impairments of the employee or applicant."[137] Title I defines reasonable accommodation to include "making existing facilities used by employees readily accessible to and usable by individuals with disabilities; . . . and job restructuring, part-time or modified work schedules, reassignment to a vacant position, acquisition or modification of equipment or devices, appropriate adjustment or modifications of examinations, training materials or policies, the provision of qualified readers or interpreters, and other similar accommodations for individuals with disabilities."[138]

An employer does not have to provide an accommodation that would be an undue hardship (defined as an action that would require significant difficulty or expense)[139] or would pose a direct threat to the health or safety of others in the workplace.[140]

The Rehabilitation Act relates to employment for federal employees. Section 501 requires affirmative action and nondiscrimination in employment by Federal agencies of the executive branch.[141] Section 503 requires affirmative action and prohibits employment discrimination by Federal government contractors and subcontractors with contracts of more than $10,000.[142] The regulations provide that the "Federal Government shall be a model employer of individuals with disabilities. Agencies shall give full consideration to the hiring, placement, and advancement of qualified individuals with disabilities."[143]

Employees of state agencies are covered under both Title I (and perhaps Title II) of the ADA, as well as Section 504 of the Rehabilitation Act, which prohibits discrimination on the basis of disability for entities that receive federal funding. Regarding employment discrimination, however, individuals may only sue state employers for prospective injunctive relief (using *Ex Parte Young*)[144] under Title I of the ADA.[145] There is currently a split as to whether individuals can sue state employers for damages for disability discrimination under the Rehabilitation Act.[146]

Regarding workplace safety issues, U.S. employees reached by Congress' interstate commerce power are protected from hazards that present significant risks of material health impairment in the workplace under the Occupational Safety and Health Act (OSHA).[147] Employers are required to comply with safety rules promulgated pursuant to OSHA.[148]

All alleged violations of ADA employment provisions must be filed with the EEOC, which is charged with investigating these complaints and finding remedies. Possible remedies include hiring, reinstatement, promotion, back pay, front pay, restored benefits, reasonable accommodation, attorneys' fees, expert witness fees, and court costs. Violations of the employment provisions of the Rehab Act by federal contractors and subcontractors can be reported to the Office of Federal Contract Compliance Programs (OFCCP) of the U.S. Department of Labor. The OFCCP will investigate and remedy violations similar to those procedures carried out by the EEOC. In addition to administrative support from EEOC, the United States has a network of

Protection and Advocacy (P&A) systems and Client Assistance Programs (CAP) for individuals with disabilities. Each state is appropriated funding from the federal budget, in combination with state and private funding, to implement and administer a P&A/CAP system. P&As provide legal representation and other advocacy services, under all federal and state laws, to all people with disabilities. CAPs provide information and assistance to individuals seeking or receiving vocational rehabilitation . . . services under the Rehabilitation Act, including assistance in pursuing administrative, legal and other appropriate remedies.

The Workforce Investment Act of 1998 (WIA) establishes state and local Workforce Investment Boards responsible for developing a "one-stop" delivery system of accessible, innovative, and comprehensive employment services.[149] They partner with local vocational rehabilitation agencies, businesses, and job training and education programs to assist local communities in increasing employment. The one-stop system also provides assistance in job search activities, career planning, job skill assessments and training, and childcare resources. One-stops also provide resources for job and entrepreneurial training, transportation and housing assistance, and access to affordable health coverage.

Among working Americans with disabilities, almost one-fifth have no health insurance coverage, largely because their incomes (though low by most standards) exceed Medicaid eligibility levels and their employers do not offer coverage. The Ticket to Work And Work Incentives Improvement Act ("TWWIIA") was passed to address this and other issues. TWIAA provides benefits to eligible individuals with disabilities who want to and are capable of working.[150] One benefit allows working individuals with disabilities the option of maintaining Medicaid health insurance coverage. This promotes the ability of participants to return to work without the loss of essential health care benefits.

TWWIIA's Ticket to Work and Self-Sufficiency Program provides recipients of disability insurance with a "ticket" to purchase employment training services from qualified Employment Networks (ENs). The goal is to encourage individuals with disabilities to seek employment rehabilitation services that aid in attaining employment and to reduce dependence on governmental benefit programs. Ticket program services include the provision of case management, workplace accommodations, peer mentoring, job training, and transportation assistance. ENs receive payment from SSA when they succeed in placing the participant in employment. Public and private organizations may apply to be ENs, as may family and friends who meet the

EN qualifications. To date, more than one-third of the states have implemented TWWIIA and others have passed legislation creating similar programs.

Article 28 of the CRPD and Description of Corresponding United States Law

ARTICLE 28 – ADEQUATE STANDARD OF LIVING AND SOCIAL PROTECTION

1. States Parties recognize the right of persons with disabilities to an adequate standard of living for themselves and their families, including adequate food, clothing and housing, and to the continuous improvement of living conditions, and shall take appropriate steps to safeguard and promote the realization of this right without discrimination on the basis of disability.
2. States Parties recognize the right of persons with disabilities to social protection and to the enjoyment of that right without discrimination on the basis of disability, and shall take appropriate steps to safeguard and promote the realization of this right, including measures:
   (a) To ensure equal access by persons with disabilities to clean water services, and to ensure access to appropriate and affordable services, devices and other assistance for disability-related needs;
   (b) To ensure access by persons with disabilities, in particular women and girls with disabilities and older persons with disabilities, to social protection programmes and poverty reduction programmes;
   (c) To ensure access by persons with disabilities and their families living in situations of poverty to assistance from the State with disability-related expenses, including adequate training, counselling, financial assistance and respite care;
   (d) To ensure access by persons with disabilities to public housing programmes;
   (e) To ensure equal access by persons with disabilities to retirement benefits and programmes.

Coverage of United States Law

Persons with disabilities are protected by the ADA and the Rehabilitation Act from discrimination in respect to the provision of government services, including equal access to social assistance, clean water, assistive devices, public housing, and retirement benefits, so long as the provision of such services does not cause a fundamental alteration to state programs providing any of those services.

The United States operates income support schemes for persons with disabilities, depending upon eligibility criteria. The largest of these programs are the Social Security Disability Insurance (SSDI) scheme that pays benefits to persons with disabilities and a limited number of family members in the event that a person who was employed and paying Social Security taxes for a sufficient amount of time becomes unable to work, and the Supplemental Security Income program that provides benefits to disabled persons on the basis of financial need.[151] Although these schemes differ in their eligibility criteria, each requires recipients to meet medically-based standards.[152]

Article 29 of the CRPD and Description of Corresponding United States Law

ARTICLE 29 – PARTICIPATION IN POLITICAL AND PUBLIC LIFE

States Parties shall guarantee to persons with disabilities their political rights and the opportunity to enjoy them on an equal basis with others, and shall undertake to:

(a) Ensure that persons with disabilities can effectively and fully participate in political and public life on an equal basis with others, directly or through freely chosen representatives, including the right and opportunity for persons with disabilities to vote and be elected, inter alia, by:

(i) Ensuring that voting procedures, facilities and materials are appropriate, accessible and easy to understand and use;

(ii) Protecting the right of persons with disabilities to vote by secret ballot in elections and public referendums, without intimidation, and to stand for elections and to effectively hold office and perform all public functions at all levels of government, facilitating the use of assistive and new technologies where appropriate;

(iii) Guaranteeing the free expression of the will of persons with disabilities as electors and to this end, where necessary, at their request, allowing assistance in voting by a person of their own choice.

(b) Promote actively an environment in which persons with disabilities can effectively and fully participate in the conduct of public affairs, without discrimination and on an equal basis with others, and encourage their participation in public affairs, including:

(i) Participation in non-governmental organizations and associations concerned with the public and political life of the country, and in the activities and administration of political parties;

(ii) Forming and joining organizations of persons with disabilities to represent persons with disabilities at international, national, regional and local levels.

Coverage of United States Law

Under United States constitutional law, voting is a "fundamental right," meaning that government infringements on the right to vote are subject to strict scrutiny. However, there is no developed body of constitutional law protecting the right of people with disabilities to vote in polling places, or secretly and independently, in part because courts have not typically applied strict scrutiny to claims involving the right to vote in a particular manner.[153] The one exception is in cases involving blanket disenfranchisement of people with certain mental disabilities.[154]

There are several United States statutes that deal with disability and political participation, particularly as it involves voting. There are three pre-ADA laws that address voting and disability. The Voting Rights Act of 1965 (amended in 1982), provides that any voter who requires assistance to vote by reason of blindness or other disability may be given assistance by a person of the voter's choice, other than the voter's employer or agent of that employer or officer or agent of the voter's union. This statute applies only to federal elections. The Voting Accessibility for the Elderly and Handicapped Act provides that "[w]ithin each State . . . each political subdivision responsible for conducting elections shall assure that all polling places for Federal elections are accessible to handicapped and elderly voters."[155] This statute, which does not purport to define "accessibility," also applies only to federal elections. Section 504 of the Rehabilitation Act of 1973,[156] prohibiting discrimination on the basis of disability in programs or activities receiving Federal financial assistance, applies to elections.

There are two provisions in the ADA that address voting, although not directly.[157] First, courts have uniformly held that voting is a "service, program, or activity" for purposes of Title II, which prohibits discrimination by public entities.[158] This means that the voting systems offered by public entities, when viewed in their entirety, must be readily accessible to and usable by people with disabilities, unless to do so would result in a fundamental alteration or cause an undue financial administrative burden (the "program access" standard). Second, Title III of the ADA, prohibiting discrimination on the basis of disability in privately owned places of public accommodation, is also relevant to voting. Some structures used for polling places--such as schools and recreational centers are covered by Title III independent of their use as polling places.

The most actively litigated area in voting and disability has been the program access standard of ADA Title II and the Rehabilitation Act. These cases fall into three categories. The first category involves cases challenging physically inaccessible polling places.[159] The second category of cases involves cases arguing that Title II requires secret and independent voting opportunities for people with disabilities. The cases have split on this issue.[160] The third category of cases involves challenges to curtailment of voting opportunities for people with mental disabilities.[161]

The last federal law impacting the voting rights of people with disabilities is the Help America Vote Act (HAVA).[162] Amongst other things, HAVA provides funds to make polling places, including the path of travel, entrances, exits, and voting areas of each polling facility, accessible to individuals with disabilities, in a manner that provides the same opportunities for access and participation (including privacy and independence) as for other voters.[163] HAVA also provides a that voting systems shall be accessible for individuals with disabilities, including non-visual accessibility for the blind and visually impaired, in a manner that provides the same opportunity for access and participation (including privacy and independence) as for other voters.[164]

Finally, in terms of organizations dedicated to promoting the role of people with disabilities in the political process, the National Council on Disability is a an independent federal agency charged with making recommendations to the President and Congress to enhance the quality of life for all Americans with disabilities and their families.

Article 30 of the CRPD and Description of Corresponding United States Law

ARTICLE 30 – PARTICIPATION IN CULTURAL LIFE, RECREATION, LEISURE, AND SPORT

1. States Parties recognize the right of persons with disabilities to take part on an equal basis with others in cultural life, and shall take all appropriate measures to ensure that persons with disabilities:
   (a) Enjoy access to cultural materials in accessible formats;
   (b) Enjoy access to television programmes, films, theatre, and other cultural activities, in accessible formats;
   (c) Enjoy access to places for cultural performances or services, such as theatres, museums, cinemas, libraries and tourism services, and, as far as possible, enjoy access to monuments and sites of national cultural importance.
2. States Parties shall take appropriate measures to enable persons with disabilities to have the opportunity to develop and utilize their creative, artistic and intellectual potential, not only for their own benefit, but also for the enrichment of society.
3. States Parties shall take all appropriate steps, in accordance with international law, to ensure that laws protecting intellectual property rights do not constitute an unreasonable or discriminatory barrier to access by persons with disabilities to cultural materials.
4. Persons with disabilities shall be entitled, on an equal basis with others, to recognition and support of their specific cultural and linguistic identity, including sign languages and deaf culture.
5. With a view to enabling persons with disabilities to participate on an equal basis with others in recreational, leisure and sporting activities, States Parties shall take appropriate measures:
   (a) To encourage and promote the participation, to the fullest extent possible, of persons with disabilities in mainstream sporting activities at all levels;

(b) To ensure that persons with disabilities have an opportunity to organize, develop and participate in disability-specific sporting and recreational activities, and to this end, encourage the provision, on an equal basis with others, of appropriate instruction, training and resources;
(c) To ensure that persons with disabilities have access to sporting and recreational and tourism venues;
(d) To ensure that children with disabilities have equal access to participation in play, recreation, and leisure and sporting activities, including those activities in the school system;
(e) To ensure that persons with disabilities have access to services from those involved in the organization of recreational, tourism, leisure and sporting activities.

Coverage of United States Law

United States domestic law has several provisions that prevent discrimination against people with disabilities in cultural life, recreation, leisure, and sport. Many such activities take place at privately owned places of public accommodation – that is, privately owned businesses or establishments that open themselves up to the public – and are covered by Title III of the ADA.[165] As such, the owners and operators cannot discriminate in the full and equal enjoyment of the goods, services, facilities, privileges, advantages, or accommodations.[166]

Title III's reach has therefore extended significantly into recreation and cultural opportunities for people with disabilities. The organizers of sports and recreation activities must make reasonable accommodations unless such accommodation would fundamentally alter the nature of the goods or services being provided.[167] Thus, for example, the Professional Golf Association had to provide a golf cart as a reasonable accommodation to a professional golfer to allow him to participate in tournament play.[168] A requested accommodation also does not have to made if it causes a direct threat to the health or safety of others.[169] Title III has beenapplied to sports leagues; i.e., its coverage is not limited to actual locations.[170]

As discussed above, pursuant to the Telecommunications Act of 1996,[171] the Federal Communications Commission has adopted rules requiring closed captioning of most, though not all, television programming.

Similarly, as with any Title III covered entity, facilities that house cultural and recreational opportunities have accessibility obligations. Facilities that predate the ADA must be accessible to the extent that doing so is "readily achievable," and new facilities (and modifications to existing facilities) must be more fully accessible to people with disabilities in accordance with the ADAAG standards. The accessibility of entertainment venues (sports stadiums and movie theatres) has been a heavily litigated area. In particular, there have been several "line of sight" cases, involving the issue of whether people who used wheelchairs are entitled to seats where they can see over people who stand in the rows in front of them.[172] Another frequently litigated issue is whether wheelchair seating in stadium-style movie theaters must offer choices of position within the theater, and to what extent wheelchair seating must be integrated into the stadium seating section of the theater.[173]

Some of the parties that control and manage recreational opportunities are public entities; for example, public parks and high school athletic associations. Therefore, Title II of the ADA and Section 504 of the Rehabilitation Act (to the extent these entities receive federal funds) are relevant as well. A public entities' obligations regarding recreation opportunities under Title II and Section 504 closely track those of private operators of places of public accommodation: they cannot discriminate on the basis of disability in their operations (which includes a duty to provide reasonable accommodation), and must make their facilities accessible.[174] One frequently litigated issue in this area involves public sports associations' role as standard-setters for who gets to participate in high school athletics.[175]

Article 31 of the CRPD and Description of Corresponding United States Law

ARTICLE 31 – STATISTICS AND DATA COLLECTION

1. States Parties undertake to collect appropriate information, including statistical and research data, to enable them to formulate and implement policies to give effect to the present Convention. The process of collecting and maintaining this information shall:
   (a) Comply with legally established safeguards, including legislation on data protection, to ensure confidentiality and respect for the privacy of persons with disabilities;

(b) Comply with internationally accepted norms to protect human rights and fundamental freedoms and ethical principles in the collection and use of statistics.

2. The information collected in accordance with this article shall be disaggregated, as appropriate, and used to help assess the implementation of States Parties' obligations under the present Convention and to identify and address the barriers faced by persons with disabilities in exercising their rights.
3. States Parties shall assume responsibility for the dissemination of these statistics and ensure their accessibility to persons with disabilities and others.

Coverage of United States Law

The United States government collects, maintains, and disseminates statistics and data relating to people with disabilities through a number of federal agencies and programs. The most comprehensive of these studies emanate from the United States Census Bureau, often in collaboration with other agencies such as the Bureau of Labor Statistics, and include the American Community Survey,[176] Census 2000,[177] and the Current Population Survey (1981-2004).[178] Additional data sources from the Federal government include the National Health Interview Survey,[179] the National Health Interview Survey - Disability Supplement,[180] and the Survey of Income and Program Participation.[181]

In addition, the United States government sponsors the collection, maintenance, and dissemination of statistics and data relating to people with disabilities through research grants. For example, the United States Department of Education, *National Institute on Disability and Rehabilitation Research* (NIDRR) funds the Cornell University ILR School Employment and Disability Institute[182] which in addition to generating national and international data and policy-based research[183] and technical assistance and training,[184] also maintains an online source for United States disability statistics,[185] produces an annual Disability Status Report,[186] and compiles the Longitudinal Study of the Vocational Rehabilitation Services Program.[187] NIDRR funding also sustains the University of California, San Francisco Disability Statistics Center,[188] co-sponsors with the Coleman Institute for Cognitive Disabilities a Rehabilitation Engineering Research Center for the

Advancement of Cognitive Technologies,[189] and enables other centers that collect disability-related data and conduct acresearch.[190]

Other United States funded initiatives include the United States Social Security Administration's support of the Program for Disability Research (a unit of the Disability Research Institute at the University of Illinois at Urbana-Champaign and a constituent unit of the School of Management and Labor Relations at Rutgers, The State University of New Jersey),[191] as well as a consortium of agencies, led by the National Science Foundation, that fund the longitudinal Panel Study of Income Dynamics,[192] among others.[193]

There are myriad regulations that govern the use of human subjects in research – which may be applicable to the collection of data and statistics. Most notably is Title 45 C.F.R. 46.101 which is followed by the U.S. Department of Health and Human Services, as well as other federal entities including the National Science Foundation, and the Departments of Energy, Transportation, and Veteran's Affairs. Although each agency has its own set of Federal Codes, the DHHS 45 CFR 46 encompasses the United States' government policies on human subjects protection. The laws apply to any research "... supported or otherwise subject to regulation by any federal department or agency..."[194] In addition, federal regulations require additional protections for children involved in research.[195]

Privacy protections relating to the collection, use, and dissemination of statistics and data are discussed in the contexts of other articles, for example *supra* Article 22.

The accessibility of these statistics and data sets are discussed in the contexts of other articles, for example, *supra* Article 9.

Article 32 of the CRPD and Description of Corresponding United States Law

ARTICLE 32 – INTERNATIONAL COOPERATION

1. States Parties recognize the importance of international cooperation and its promotion, in support of national efforts for the realization of the purpose and objectives of the present Convention, and will undertake appropriate and effective measures in this regard, between and among States and, as appropriate, in partnership with relevant international and regional organizations and civil society, in particular

organizations of persons with disabilities. Such measures could include, inter alia:

(a) Ensuring that international cooperation, including international development programmes, is inclusive of and accessible to persons with disabilities;
(b) Facilitating and supporting capacity-building, including through the exchange and sharing of information, experiences, training programmes and best practices;
(c) Facilitating cooperation in research and access to scientific and technical knowledge;
(d) Providing, as appropriate, technical and economic assistance, including by facilitating access to and sharing of accessible and assistive technologies, and through the transfer of technologies.

2. The provisions of this article are without prejudice to the obligations of each State Party to fulfill its obligations under the present Convention.

Coverage of United States Law

The United States Department of State provides some amount of technical assistance to foreign governments on their disability laws and policies, and also assesses the extent of disability rights and exclusion in foreign governments as part of its annual human rights reports.[196] These Country Reports on Human Rights Practices are in turn submitted annually to Congress in compliance with sections 116(d) and 502B(b) of the Foreign Assistance Act of 1961, as amended, and section 504 of the Trade Act of 1974, as amended.[197] Although progress has been made in including a section on disability in these reports, the depth of the reporting is still lacking.

A recent initiative funded by the United States Agency for International Development (USAID) seeks to address the integration of disability issues into the programming of large humanitarian assistance organizations.[198] This builds on USAID's incremental efforts to integrate a disability dimension in its foreign assistance programming.[199]

Articles 33-40 of CRPD and Description of Corresponding United States Law

Articles 33-40 deal with the implementation and monitoring of the treaty by states parties. Accordingly, this section will discuss the existing schemes of implementation and enforcement for the major federal disability laws.

Coverage of United States Law

The enforcement of U.S. civil rights law is usually decentralized, with some balance between private and public enforcement. In private enforcement schemes, individuals can sue to vindicate their statutory rights, typically either for damages and/or an injunction. In public enforcement schemes, some part of the federal government is authorized to bring suits in the public interest for statutory violations. To varying extents, the different disability law statues are a blend of each.

Americans with Disabilities Act

Aggrieved individuals are allowed to file suit under Title I of the ADA. Before they do so, they must file their claim with the Equal Employment Opportunity Commission (EEOC). The basic rule is that they have 180 days to do so.[200] The EEOC finds that "there is reasonable cause to believe that an unlawful practice has occurred or is occurring,"[201] it will attempt to conciliate with the employer. If the EEOC does not resolve the matter, it will either issue a determination that reasonable cause exists to believe that an unlawful practice has occurred, or find that there is not reasonable cause to believe that an unlawful practice has occurred and issue a "right to sue" letter. The EEOC is authorized to bring a civil action on the individual's behalf, unless the employer is a government, governmental agency, or political subdivision, in which case the EEOC refers the matter to the Attorney General who can initiate a civil action.[202] The EEOC, responsible for enforcing Title I against private employers, has the ability to be bring suit as a plaintiff, and its claims are not limited to the complaints made by a charging party.[203] Within 90 days of receiving a right to sue letter, an individual may bring a civil action for violation of the statute.

The default remedy under Title I of the ADA for intentional discrimination is equitable – enjoining the respondent from continuing to engage in the unlawful employment action and ordering reinstatement or hiring, as the case may be. As an adjunct to reinstatement or hiring, the court may order back pay or other appropriate equitable relief. The time period for back pay is limited to two years. In the event reinstatement is not appropriate, the court may order front pay. The Civil Rights Act, from which the ADA remedial scheme is derived, imposes monetary limitations on damage awards, depending on the size of the employer. In addition, an injured party may receive other compensatory damages, including damages for future pecuniary losses, emotional pain, suffering, inconvenience, mental anguish, loss of enjoyment of life, and other non-pecuniary losses, as well as punitive damages when the defendant acts with malice or with reckless indifference to the federally protected rights of an aggrieved individual.

Title II of the ADA and Section 504 of the Rehabilitation Act have public and private enforcement mechanisms. An individual may sue in federal court, generally without exhausting any administrative remedies. In terms of remedies, Title II provides that "[t]he remedies, procedures, and rights set forth in section 505 of the Rehabilitation Act of 1973 shall be the remedies, procedures, and rights that this title provides to any person alleging discrimination on the basis of disability in violation of section 202."[204] Section 505, however, does not contain any remedies provisions. As a result of this ambiguity, courts have had to develop case law about the specific remedies available to private individuals in Title II cases. Although the case law is not crystal clear, several principles have emerged. First, individuals may receive injunctive relief for Title II violations. The only possible exception to this rule is in suits against states, which may trigger sovereign immunity federalism issues limiting the availability of certain types of injunctive relief. At a minimum, an individual or the federal government may receive prospective injunctive relief under the doctrine of *Ex Parte Young*.

Another general rule is that plaintiffs may recover compensatory damages in Title II cases. This includes damages for emotional distress, pain and suffering, and economic loss. This general rule is subject to two important qualifications. First, after *Tennessee v. Lane*,[205] an individual's ability to recover damages from a violating state employer depends on whether or not that individual is suing to vindicate a "fundamental right." If the right is "fundamental," Title II of the ADA is viewed as a valid waiver of the states' sovereign immunity, and damages are allowed. the right is not "fundamental," courts are split on whether Title II validly abrogates state sovereign immunity and, therefore, allows for damages. The second qualification to a plaintiff's ability to recover compensatory damages depends on whether the discrimination complained of is the result of the disparate impact of facially neutral actions or discriminatory intent. Although there is not complete uniformity, a consensus among courts has developed that a plaintiff seeking compensatory damages must show that the defendant has intentionally discriminated, as opposed to engaging in a practice that has a discriminatory effect. In order to recover damages, the plaintiff must show that the defendant acted with at least "deliberate indifference."[206] The entity must know that an accommodation is required and must fail to make the accommodation in a way that bespeaks more than negligence and has an element of deliberateness, by, for example, failing to consider an individual's needs. In *Barnes v. Gorman*,[207] the Supreme Court held that punitive damages are not available in Title II cases.

Under Title II, private individuals may also pursue administrative remedies, which may ultimately lead to DOJ involvement. Within 180 days of the violation, an individual must file a complaint with any appropriate agency or the DOJ.[208] Subpart G of the DOJ Title II regulations designates different agencies that exercise responsibilities, regulate, or administer services, programs, or activities in specified areas.[209] These agencies are the Departments of Agriculture, Education, Health and Human Services, Housing and Urban Development, Interior, Justice, Labor, and Transportation. All designated agencies (including the DOJ) must investigate a complaint and attempt informal resolution. If this fails, the agency issues findings of fact and conclusions of law, a description of the appropriate remedy, and a notice to the complainant and public entity. If it finds noncompliance, it issues a letter of noncompliance, notifies the Assistant Attorney General in charge of the Civil Rights Division of the DOJ, and attempts to negotiate to secure compliance. If that fails, the matter is referred to the Assistant Attorney General for litigation.

Title III is also enforceable by private parties. Title III, however, does not provide a damage remedy for private litigants. The relevant provision states that the "remedies and procedures set forth in section 204(a) of the Civil Rights Act of 1964 are the remedies and procedures this title provides to any person who is being subjected to discrimination on the basis of disability in violation of this title."[210] The referenced remedies in the Civil Rights Act of 1964 only include prospective injunctive relief.

Title III gives the DOJ broader powers than individual litigants. The DOJ can investigate complaints, and it may commence a civil action if it believes that any person or group of persons is engaged in a pattern or practice of discrimination, or any person or group of persons has been discriminated against and such discrimination raises an issue of general public importance.[211] The DOJ is also authorized to obtain compensatory damages in addition to the equitable relief available when individuals sue on their own behalf.[212] In cases the DOJ deems important to "vindicate the public interest," it may also seek civil penalties (not to exceed $50,000 for the first violation and $100,000 for subsequent violations).[213] The DOJ can choose to litigate cases, obtain consent decrees, or settle.

Individuals with Disabilities Education Act

The IDEA is a federal funding statute, meaning federal funding is conditioned on compliance and funding can be revoked by the federal government if noncompliance is found. However, students with disabilities also have a private right of action to enforce the IDEA through the special education process. Parents who successfully challenge inadequate IEPs may be entitled to declaratory and injunctive relief directing the state to provide FAPE. They may also be entitled to reimbursement for their out-of-pocket expenses, including private school tuition.[214] A student may also be entitled to compensatory educational services to remedy past failures to provide FAPE.[215]

The IDEA does not specify what relief is available, and the circuits have split on the issue of whether tort-like compensatory damages are available under the IDEA or under 42 U.S.C. § 1983 to enforce IDEA rights. The Fourth, Sixth, Seventh, Eighth, Ninth, Tenth, and Eleventh circuits have found damages unavailable.[216] However, some circuits have found damages to be available under 42 U.S.C. § 1983 for violations of the IDEA.[217]

Sovereign immunity limits the availability of damages from state governments, and punitive damages are generally not available against government agencies. *See* Barnes v. Gorman, 536 U.S. 181, 189 (2002).

Parents who prevail in an IDEA administrative or judicial proceeding are entitled to reasonable attorneys' fees, in the court's discretion.[218] No multiplier of fees is permitted.[219] Fees may not be awarded for attorney participation in IEP Team meetings.[220] The Supreme Court has also recently held that parents cannot recover non-attorney expert fees in IDEA cases.[221]

Help America Vote Act

The Help America Vote Act provides that that voting systems shall "be accessible for individuals with disabilities, including nonvisual accessibility for the blind and visually impaired, in a manner that provides the same opportunity for access and participation (including privacy and independence) as for other voters."[222] There is no express private right of action for this provision in HAVA. The only grievance option available to private citizens is an administrative proceeding. The DOJ has taken the position that individuals do not have a private right of action to enforce this part of HAVA.[223] The DOJ does have the ability under HAVA to bring "civil actions against any State or jurisdiction in an appropriate United States District Court for such declaratory and injunctive relief as may be necessary."[224]

Civil Rights of Institutionalized Persons Act

The Civil Rights of Institutionalized Persons Act (CRIPA)[225] authorizes the U.S. Attorney General to investigate conditions of confinement at State and local government institutions such as prisons, jails, pretrial detention centers, juvenile correctional facilities, publicly operated nursing homes, and institutions for people with psychiatric or developmental disabilities. Its purpose is to allow the Attorney General to uncover and correct widespread deficiencies that seriously jeopardize the health and safety of residents of institutions. The Attorney General may initiate civil law suits where there is reasonable cause to believe that conditions are "egregious or flagrant," that they are subjecting residents to "grievous harm," and that they are part of a "pattern or practice" of resistance to residents' full enjoyment of constitutional or Federal rights, including title II of the ADA and section 504 of the Rehabilitation Act.

Fair Housing Amendments Act

The FHAA can be enforced in several ways. First, an aggrieved individual can bring a direct complaint in federal district or state court.[226] There is no requirement that a plaintiff exhaust her administrative remedies prior to filing suit. The statue of limitations is two years. Courts are authorized to appoint attorneys for persons alleging discriminatory housing practices (or persons against whom such a practice is alleged), or allow them to file a civil action without paying fees or costs, if, in the opinion of the court, such person is financially unable to bear the costs of such action.[227] Courts are also authorized to award actual and punitive damages, and grant other relief as the court deems appropriate, including temporary inunctions, temporary restraining orders, or permanent orders.[228] It is worth noting that this is quite different from ADA Title III's remedial scheme, which makes no provision for compensatory or punitive damages. Under the FHA, it is within the court's discretion to award attorneys' fees to a prevailing plaintiff (except for the United States). The Attorney General may intervene in a private action.[229]

The FHAA also contemplates an administrative remedy scheme, through a complaint to HUD.[230] These actions have the advantage of expedited discovery and hearings, and actual damages and civil penalties up to $50,000 can be awarded, and attorneys' fees.[231] Finally, the Attorney General may bring action in cases where there appears to be a pattern or practice of resistance to compliance with the Act.[232]

The National Council on Disability wishes to express its appreciation to Professor Michael Stein, Executive Director of the Harvard Project on Disability, and Associate Professor Michael Waterstone, Loyola Law School Los Angeles, who co-authored this paper.

End Notes

[1] 42 U.S.C. § 4151-4157
[2] 29 U.S.C. § 791 *et. seq.*
[3] 20 U.S.C. § 1400 *et. seq.*
[4] 42 U.S.C. § 1973aa-6
[5] 42 U.S.C. §§ 1973ee *et seq.*
[6] 42 U.S.C.A. § 15301 *et. seq.*
[7] 49 U.S.C. § 41705
[8] 42 U.S.C. § 3604(f).
[9] 42 U.S.C. § 12101 *et. seq.*
[10] 42 U.S.C. § 12181(a).
[11] *Id.* at (b).
[12] 42 U.S.C. § 12102(1)
[13] The ADA regulations, define auxiliary aides and services as including "[q]ualified interpreters, notetakers, transcription services, written materials, telephone handset amplifiers, assistive listening devices, assistive listening systems, telephones compatible with hearing aids, closed caption decoders, open and closed captioning, telecommunications devices for deaf persons (TDD's), videotext displays, or other effective methods of making aurally delivered materials available to individuals with hearing impairments; qualified readers, taped texts, audio recordings, Brailled materials, large print materials, or other effective methods of making visually delivered materials available to individuals with visual impairments; acquisition or modification of equipment or devices; and other similar services and actions. 28 C.F.R. § 35.104(a).

[14] 42 U.S.C. § 12112(a) (emphasis added). There are additional statutory provisions spelling out what constitutes discrimination in additional detail. *See* 42 U.S.C. § 12112(b).
[15] 42 U.S.C. § 12111(8).
[16] 42 U.S.C. § 12132.
[17] 42 U.S.C. § 12182(a). Title III also contains additional statutory provisions providing more detail to this general prohibition. *See* 42 U.S.C. § 12182(b).
[18] 42 U.S.C. § 12111.
[19] 480 U.S. 273 (1987).
[20] *Id.* at 287, n.17.
[21] 480 U.S. 273 (1987).
[22] *See* 28 C.F.R. § 35.130(b)(7).
[23] 42 U.S.C. § 12182(b)(2)(a)(ii).
[24] 42 U.S.C. § 12102(2).
[25] *See, e.g.,* National Council on Disability, *Righting the ADA* (Dec., 2004).
[26] U.S. Const., XIV Amendment, Sec. 2.
[27] *See* City of Cleburne, Texas v. Cleburne Living Center, 473 U.S. 432 (1985).
[28] In fact, Section 501 of the Rehabilitation Act, 29 U.S.C. § 791, expressly requires affirmative action plans by Executive Branch agencies.
[29] U.S. Const., XIV Am., Sec.5.
[30] 42 U.S.C. § 2000e-2.
[31] 42 U.S.C. § 2000e-2(e).
[32] Meritor Savings Bank v. Vinson, 477 U.S. 57, 67 (1986).
[33] 20 U.S.C. §§ 1681-83, 1685, 1686.
[34] *See* Troxel v. Granville, 530 U.S. 57, 84 n.5 (2000) (Stevens, J, dissenting).
[35] *See, e.g.* Washington v. Indiana High School Athletic Association, 181 F.3d 840, 852 (7th Cir. 1999) (high school athletic association must accommodate school age child in sporting activities); Dennin v. Connecticut Interscholastic Athletic Assc., 913 F.Supp.663 (D. Conn. 1996) (same).
[36] *See* Board of Education v. Rowley, 458 U.S. 176 (1982).
[37] *See* Yeskey v. Pa. Dep't of Corr., 118 F.3d 168, 171 (3rd Cir. 1997) (noting that Title II's language brings within its scope "anything a public entity does."); *see also* Barden v. City of Sacramento, 292 F.3d 1073 (9th Cir. 2002) (holding that sidewalks were covered by Title II); Rodde v. Bonta, 357 F.3d 988 (9th Cir. 2004) (public hospitals covered by Title II); Parker v. Universidad de Puerto Rico, 225 F.3d 1 (2000) (public university covered by Title II).
[38] The relevant regulations define facilities as "all or any portion of buildings, structures, sites, complexes, equipment, rolling stock or other conveyances, roads, walks, passageways, parking lots, or other real or personal property, including the site where the building, property, structure, or equipment is located." 28 C.F.R. § 35.104.
[39] 28 C.F.R. § 35.151(a), (b).
[40] 42 U.S.C. § 12142.
[41] *Id.* at 12143(a).
[42] *Id.* at 12162.
[43] *See* Martin v. Metropolitan Atlanta Rapid Transit Authority, 225 F.Supp. 1362, 1377 (N.D. Ga 2002) (holding that a transit authority's website providing scheduling information for bus and other transit services must be accessible under Title II).
[44] 42 U.S.C. § 12181 *et. seq.*
[45] *See* Martin v. PGA Tour, 532 U.S. 661 (2001) (holding that the PGA Golf Tour must modify its "walking-only" rule to accommodate a golfer with a disability who needed to use a golf cart).
[46] 42 U.S.C. § 12188; *see also* Aikens v. St Helena Hospital, 843 F.Supp. 1329 (N.D. Cal. 1994) (holding that hospital might have to provide sign language interpreters, although this plaintiff's claim was dismissed for lack of standing). In the regulations, auxiliary aids and

services are defined to include "qualified interpreters, note-takers, computer aided transcription services, written materials, telephone handset amplifiers, assistive listening devices, assistive listening systems, telephones compatible with hearing aids, closed caption decoders, open and closed captioning, telecommunications devices for deaf persons (TDDs), videotext displays . . . qualified readers, taped texts, audio recordings, Brailled materials, [and] large print materials." 28 C.F.R. § 36.303(b).

[47] 42 U.S.C. § 12182(b)(2)(A)(iv); *id.* at 12181(9). The regulations list examples steps to remove barriers as "installing ramps; making curb cuts in sidewalks and entrances; repositioning shelves; rearranging tables, chairs, vending machines, display racks, and other furniture; repositioning telephones; adding raised markings on elevator control buttons; installing flashing alarm lights; widening doors; installing offset hinges to widen doorways; eliminating a turnstile or providing an alternative accessible path; installing accessible door hardware; installing grab bars in toilet stalls; rearranging toilet partitions to increase maneuvering space; insulating lavatory pipes under sinks to prevent burns; installing a raised toilet seat; installing a full-length bathroom mirror; repositioning the paper towel dispenser in a bathroom; creating designated accessible parking spaces; installing an accessible paper cup dispenser at an existing inaccessible water fountain; removing high pile, low density carpeting; or installing vehicle hand controls." 28 C.F.R. § 36.304(b).

[48] 42 U.S.C.§ 12147(a).

[49] 42 U.S.C. § 12183(a).

[50] 28 C.F.R. pt. 36, app. A. § 2.2.

[51] 42 U.S.C. § 12184.

[52] *See* Access Now, Inc. v. Southwest Airlines, Co., 227 F.Supp.2d 312 (S.D. Fla. 2002) (holding that websites without nexus are not covered by Title III); *see also* National Federation of the Blind v. Target Corporation, 452 F.Supp.2d 946 (N.D. Cal. 2006) (same, but also holding that website that does have a nexus to actual place of public accommodation does have to be accessible).

[53] *Id.*

[54] *See* Shapiro v. Cadman Towers, Inc., 51 F.3d 328 (2nd Cir. 1995) (holding that an owner of an apartment building had to make an exception for tenant with multiple sclerosis in parking space policy); *see also* United States v. Freer, 864 F.Supp. 324 (W.D.N.Y. 1994) (holding owners of trailer park in violation of FHAA where owners refused to allow renter to install desired wheelchair ramp at her own cost).

[55] These include that "the public use and common use portions of such dwellings are readily accessible to and usable by handicapped persons; all the doors designed to allow passage into and within all premises within such dwellings are sufficiently wide to allow passage by handicapped persons in wheelchairs; and all premises within such dwellings contain the following features of adaptive design: an accessible route into and through the dwelling; light switches, electrical outlets, thermostats, and other environmental controls in accessible locations; reinforcements in bathroom walls to allow later installation of grab bars; and usable kitchens and bathrooms such that an individual in a wheelchair can maneuver about the space." 42 U.S.C. § 3604(f)(3)(c).

[56] *Cf. The Oregon Health Care Proposal and the Americans with Disabilities Act*, 106 HARV. L. REV. 1296 (1993) (asserting that the proposal withstands ADA scrutiny).

[57] For a discussion, *see* JOSEPH P. SHAPIRO, NO PITY: PEOPLE WITH DISABILITIES FORGING A NEW CIVIL RIGHTS MOVEMENT 324-28 (1993); Michael Ashley Stein, *From Crippled to Disabled: The Legal Empowerment of Americans with Disabilities,* 43 EMORY L.J. 247, 266-67 (1994).

[58] For a thoughtful discussion of these cases, and especially the role that disability rights advocates play within their parameters, see Samuel R. Bagenstos, *Disability, Life, Death, and Choice*, 29 HARV. J. L. & GENDER 425 (2006).

[59] The best known of these instances, the "Baby Doe" cases, are discussed in U.S. Comm'n on Civil Rights, *Medical Discrimination Against Children with Disabilities* (1989); *see also*

MARTHA MINOW, MAKING ALL THE DIFFERENCE: INCLUSION, EXCLUSION, AND AMERICAN LAW 328-33 (1990).

[60] *See, e.g.,* Bowen v. Am. Hosp. Ass'n., 476 U.S. 610 (1986) (ruling against the use of Rehabilitation Act regulation that would prohibit hospitals from withholding treatment from infants with disabilities in the future); United States v. Univ. Hosp., State Univ. of NY, at Stony Brook, 729 F.2d 144 (2d Cir. 1984) (holding that the Rehabilitation Act was not apposite to circumstances involving the withholding of medical treatment).

[61] *See* Washington v. Glucksburg, 521 U.S. 702 (1997); Vacco v. Quinn, 521 U.S. 793 (1997).

[62] *See* Gonzales v. Oregon, 126 S.Ct. 904 (2006).

[63] This is especially true when guardians make these determinations on behalf of incapacitated persons with disabilities, as in the heavily publicized cases involving Nancy Beth Cruzan, Karen Ann Quinlan, and Terri Schaivo. *See* National Council on Disability, *Assisted Suicide: A Disability Perspective* (March, 1997), *available online at* <http://www.ncd.gov/newsroom/publications/1997/suicide.htm>.

[64] *See* National Council on Disability Public Consultation, *Homeland Security, Emergency Preparedness, Disaster Relief and Recovery* (May, 2007), *available online at* <http://www.ncd.gov/newsroom/publications/2007/ncd_consultant_05-31-07.htm >.

[65] 473 U.S. 432 (1985).

[66] *Id.* at 441.

[67] *See* Pennsylvania v. Yeskey, 524 U.S. 206 (1998) (state prisons fall within coverage of Title II); *see also* Tennessee v. Lane, 541 U.S. 509 (2004) (courts); Galloway v. Sup. Ct. of D.C., 816 F.Supp. 12 (D.D.C. 1993) (state and municipal courts); Gorman v. Bartch, 152 F.3d 907 (8th Cir. 1998) (local police departments).

[68] *See* Galloway v. Superior Court of District of Columbia, 816 F.Supp.12 (D.D.C. 1993) (state policy of not allowing individuals with visual impairments to serve on juries violates ADA).

[69] *See* Matthews v. Jefferson, 29 F.Supp. 2d 525 (W.D. Ar, 1998) (holding that county violated the ADA by failing to make courthouse readily accessible to paraplegic); *see also* Layton v. Elder, 143 F.3d 469 (8th Cir. 1998) (same).

[70] *See* State v. Schaim, 600 N.E.2d 661 (Ohio 1992); *see also* State v. Rivera, 480 N.Y.S.2d 426 (N.Y. Sup. Ct. 1984).

[71] 457 U.S. 307 (1982).

[72] *Id. See also* Diane M. Weidert, *Constitutional Rights of the Involuntarily Committed Mentally Retarded After Youngberg v. Romeo,* 14 ST. MARY's L. J. 1113 (1982).

[73] 42 U.S.C. § 1997 *et seq.*

[74] *Id.* Additional information is posted on the U.S. Department of Justice Civil Rights Division Special Litigation Section website, *available online at* <http://www.usdoj.gov/crt/split/ >.

[75] 546 U.S. 151 (2006).

[76] The DOJ, for example, does support some programs to work with people with disabilities who are the victims of violence. *See* < http://www.ojp.usdoj.gov/ovc/help/disabled.htm>, and the NCD has entered into a strategic partnership with the DOJ on this issue. *See* National Council on Disability, *Joint Statement by the National Council on Disability Association of University Centers on Disabilities, and the National Center for Victims of Crime* (May 21, 2007), *available at* < http://www.ncd.gov/newsroom/publications/2007/05-21-07_jointstatement_crime.htm>.

[77] 274 U.S. 200 (1927).

[78] 42 U.S.C. § 1396(r), 42 U.S.C. § 1395 i-3.

[79] *See* U.S. Const., XIV Amend., Sec. 1, Cl. 1; *see also* U.S. Const., Art. IV, Sec. 2, Cl. 1.

[80] 473 U.S. 432 (1985).

[81] *Id.* at 441. For a critique, see Anita Silvers and Michael Ashley Stein, *Disability, Equal Protection, and the Supreme Court: Standing at the Crossroads of Progressive and Retrogressive Logic in Constitutional Classification*, 35 U. MICH. J. L. REFORM 81 (2002).

[82] 527 US 581 (1999).

[83] *Id.* at 593.
[84] *Id.* at 592, citing 28 CFR § 35.130(d).
[85] 28 C.F.R. § 35.160(a). *See* Soto v. City of Newark, 72 F.Supp.2d 489 (D.N.J. 1999) (holding that city who failed to provide sign language interpreter for hearing impaired individuals getting married in municipal court violated ADA).
[86] 28 C.F.R. § 35.160(b)(1) (2003).
[87] *Id.* at § 35.160(b)(2).
[88] *Id.* at § 35.104(a).
[89] *Id.* at § 35.104(b).
[90] *Id.* at § 35.164.
[91] *See* Petersen v. Hastings Public Schools, 31 F.3d 705 (8th Cir. 1994), (holding that plaintiff was not entitled to specific sign language system that was used in his home).
[92] *See* Martin v. Metropolitan Atlanta Rapid Transit Authority, 225 F.Supp. 1362, 1377 (N.D. Ga 2002) (holding that a transit authority's website providing scheduling information for bus and other transit services must be accessible under Title II).
[93] *See* Summary of 508 Standards, *available at* <*http://www.section508.gov/index.cfm?FuseAction=Content&ID=11* >.
[94] 42 U.S.C. § 12188.
[95] 28 C.F.R. § 36.303(b).
[96] *See* Access Now, Inc. v. Southwest Airlines, *Co*, 227 F.Supp.2d 312 (S.D. Fla. 2002) (holding that websites without nexus are not covered by Title III); *see also* National Federation of the Blind v. Target Corporation, 452 F.Supp.2d 946 (N.D. Cal. 2006) (same, but also holding that website that does have a nexus to actual place of public accommodation does have to be accessible).
[97] 47 CFR §§ 64.601 *et seq.*
[98] 47 U.S.C. § 609 *et. seq.*
[99] 29 U.S.C. § 3002.
[100] *See* WEBER, *supra* note 33.
[101] 18 U.S.C. § 245.
[102] See <http://www.fbi.gov/ucr/hc2006/table1.html >.
[103] 42 U.S.C. § 12112(d)(3)(B) ("[I]nformation obtained regarding the medical condition or history of the applicant [must be] collected and maintained on a separate forms and in separate medical files and is treated as a confidential medical record, except that (i) supervisors and managers may be informed regarding necessary restrictions of the work or duties of the employee and necessary accommodations; (ii) first aid and safety personnel may be informed, when appropriate, if the disability might require emergency treatment; and (iii) government officials investigating compliance with this chapter shall be provided relevant information on request … .").
[104] *See* Skinner v. Oklahoma, 316 U.S. 535 (1942).
[105] 274 U.S. 200 (1927).
[106] *See* Stanley v. Illinois, 405 U.S. 645 (1972); *see also* Santosky v. Kramer, 455 U.S. 745 (1982) (holding termination of parental rights must adhere to due process demands).
[107] *See* In re C.M., 2004 WL 1900100 (Iowa App. 2004) (allowing parents to oppose termination on grounds that it would violate the ADA); *see also* In re Welfare of H.S., 973 P.2d 474, 481 (Wash. App. 1999) (same).
[108] *See* Popovich v. Cuyahoga County Court, 276 F.3d 808 (6th Cir. 2002) (state must provide interpreter for hearing-impaired litigant in child custody hearing).
[109] *See, e.g.,* In re La'Asia Lanae S., 803 N.Y.S.2d 568, 569 (N.Y. App. Div. 2005) (ADA "has no bearing on" termination of parental rights proceedings"); In re Anthony P., 101 Cal.Rptr.2d 423, 425-26 (Cal. App. 2000) (termination of parental rights proceedings ar enot "services, programs, or activities" for purposes of ADA).
[110] 20 U.S.C. §1400(d) (2000).

[111] *Id.* §1412(a)(1)(A).
[112] *Id.* § 1412(a)(3)(A).
[113] *Id.* § 1412(a)(5)(A).
[114] *Id.* § 1415(j).
[115] *Id.* § 1412(a)(1)(B).
[116] *Id.* § 1401(3)(B).
[117] 334 F. Supp. 1257 (E.D. Pa. 1971).
[118] *Id.* at 1260 (emphasis added).
[119] 347 U.S. 482 (1954)
[120] *Pennsylvania,* 334 F.Supp. at 1260.
[121] 348 F. Supp. 866, 875 (D.D.C. 1972).
[122] *See* Parker v. Universidad de Puerto Rico, 225 F.3d 1 (1st Cir. 2000); *see also Washington v. Indiana High School Athletic Association*, 181 F.3d 840, 852 (7th Cir. 1999) (making reasonable modifications to athletic programs).
[123] *See* Naropa Inst., (CO) (1993) (Office of Civil Rights finding that a school violated Section 504 when it required a student to sign a document stating that the provision of interpreter for 12 credits of course work was a financial hardship to the school and that "unless we can find other sources of income ..the [school] will not be able to continue this level of service."); *see also* United States v. Board of Trustees for University of Alabama, 908 F.2d 740 (1990) (holding that requiring hearing-impaired students to show that they lacked the financial means to pay for their own interpreters and other auxiliary aides violated Section 504).
[124] 42 U.S.C. § 423(d)(2)(A).
[125] *See, e.g.,* Aikens v. St. Helena Hospital, 843 F.Supp. 1329 (N.D. Cal. 1994) (suggesting that private hospital might need to provide effective sign language interpreters under Title III of the ADA and Section 504 of the Rehabilitation Act); *see also* Majocha v. Turner, 166 F.Supp.2d 316 (W.D. Penn. 2001) (same); Olmstead v. Zimring, 527 U.S. 581 (1999) (holding that Title II of the ADA requires states to move individuals into community based settings, when appropriate, to the extent that they are able to do so and still attend to their complete population of individuals with mental disabilities); Rodde v. Bonta, 357 F.3d 988 (9th Cir. 2004) (holding that Title II prevented county from closing rehabilitation center dedicated primarily to providing inpatient and outpatient rehabilitative care to severely disabled individuals); Lovell v. Chandler, 303 F.3d 1039 (9th Cir. 2002) (holding that Title II prevented state from excluding category of people with disabilities from a Medicaid waiver program).
[126] *See, e.g.,* Alexander v. Choate, 469 U.S. 287 (1985) (holding that state's reduction in Medicaid coverage of annual inpatient hospitalization from twenty to fourteen days did not violate Section 504 of the Rehabilitation Act, despite the fact that the policy would adversely impact people with disabilities.); Meyers v. Colorado Dep't of Health Services, 2003 WL 1826166 (10th Cir. 2003) (holding that Title II does not require state to change content of health services); Smith v. Moorman, 2002 WL 31182541 (6th Cir. 2002) (same); Doe v. Pfrommer, 148 F.3d 73 (2d Cir. 1998) (same); Does 1-5 v. Chandler, 83 F.3d 1150 (9th Cir. 1996) (same).
[127] *See* Carparts Distribution Center v. Automotive Wholesaler's Association of New England, 37 F.3d 12 (1st Cir. 1994) (holding that disability insurance policy was covered under Title III); *but see* Parker v. Metropolitan Life Insurance, 121 F.3d 1006 (6th Cir. 1997) (holding that insurance policies are not covered by Title III of the ADA).
[128] "Titles I through IV of this Act shall not be construed to prohibit or restrict: (1) an insurer, hospital or medical service company, health maintenance organization, or any agent, or entity that administers benefit plans, or similar organizations from underwriting risks, classifying risks, or administering such risks that are based on or not inconsistent with State law; or (2) a person or organization covered by this Act from establishing, sponsoring, observing or administering the terms of a bona fide benefit plan that are based on

underwriting risks, classifying risks, or administering such risks that are based on or not inconsistent with State law; or (3) a person or organization covered by this Act from establishing, sponsoring, observing or administering the terms of a bona fide benefit plan that is not subject to State laws that regulate insurance. Paragraphs (1), (2), and (3) shall not be used as a subterfuge to evade the purposes of titles I and III." 42 U.S.C. § 12201(c).

[129] *See* Pallozzi v. Allstate Life Ins. Co., 198 F.3d 28, 33 (2d Cir. 2000) (holding that "an entity covered by Title III is not only obligated by the statute to provide disabled persons with physical access, but is also prohibited from refusing to sell them its merchandise by reason of discrimination against their disability.").

[130] There are a variety of reasons this happens. First, in some cases, courts reasoned that an insurance policy was not a "public accommodation" for purposes of Title III of the ADA. *See* Kolling v. Blue Cross, 318 F.3d 715 (6th Cir. 2003); *see also* Ford v. Schering-Plough Corp., 145 F.3d 601 (3d Cir. 1998). Second, courts reasoned that differentiation in insurance policies was not actionable discrimination on the basis of disability. *See* Soshinksy v. First Unum Life Ins. Co., No. 99-36187, 2001 WL 50535 (9th Cir. Jan 19, 2001); *see also* McNeil v. Time Ins. Co., 205 F.3d 179 (5th Cir. 2000); Doe v. Mut. of Omaha Ins. Co., 179 F.3d 557 (7th Cir. 1999). Third, courts found that the ADA's exemption for insurance policies applied and controlled the outcome of the case. *See* Fitts v. Nat'l. Mortgage. Ass'n, 236 F.3d 1 (D.C. Cir. 2001).

[131] 527 U.S. 581 (1999).

[132] United States v. Robel, 389 U.S. 258, 265 n.11 (1967).

[133] *See* United States v. Carolene Products Co., 304 U.S. 144, 151 (1938).

[134] *See* City of Cleburne, Texas v. Cleburne Living Center, 473 U.S. 432 (1985).

[135] 42 U.S.C. § 12112(a).

[136] *Id.* § 12111(5)(A).

[137] 42 U.S.C. § 12112(b)(5)(A-B).

[138] *Id.* § 12111(9).

[139] *See* 42 U.S.C § 12112(10)(A). According to the statute, the factors to be considered include (i) the nature and cost of the accommodation needed under this chapter; (ii) the overall financial resources of the facility or facilities involved in the provision of the reasonable accommodation; the number of persons employed at such facility; the effect on expenses and resources, or the impact otherwise of such accommodation upon the operation of the facility; (iii) the overall financial resources of the covered entity; the overall size of the business of a covered entity with respect to the number of its employees; the number, type, and location of its facilities; and (iv the type of operation or operations of the covered entity, including the composition, structure, and functions of the workforce of such entity; the geographic separateness, administrative, or fiscal relationship of the facility or facilities in question to the covered entity." *Id.* at (C)(i-iv).

[140] *See* 12111(3). *See also* Chevron v. Echazabal, 536 U.S. 75 (2002) (extending "direct threat" defense to harm to self).

[141] 29 U.S.C. § 791.

[142] *Id.* at § 793.

[143] 29 C.F.R. § 1614.203.

[144] 209 U.S. 123 (1908).

[145] *See* Board of Trustees of the University of Alabama v. Garrett, 531 U.S. 356 (2001)(holding that Congress did not validly abrogate state sovereign immunity regarding employment ADA claims, and therefore individuals can not sue states for damages).

[146] *See* Garrett v. Univ. of Alabama at Birmingham, 344 F.3d 1288 (11th Cir. 2003) (state waived sovereign immunity by accepting federal funds under Rehab Act); *but see* Purvis v. Williams, 73 P.2d 740 (2003) (Supreme Court of Kansas holding opposite).

[147] 2 U.S.C. § 1341 *et. seq.*

[148] 29 U.S.C. § 654.

[149] 29 U.S.C. § 701(b)(1).

[150] 20 C.F.R. § 411.125(b).

[151] An overview is contained in the Social Security Disability Programs webpage, *available online at* <http://www.ssa.gov/disability >.

[152] *See generally* Matthew Diller, *Entitlement and Exclusion: The Role of Disability in the Social Welfare System*, 44 UCLA L. REV. 361 (1996).

[153] *See generally* Michael Waterstone, *Constitutional and Statutory Voting Rights for People with Disabilities*, 14 STAN. LAW & POLICY REVIEW 353 (2003).

[154] *See* Doe v. Roe, 156 F.Supp.2d 35 (D. Me. 2001) (striking down such a state statute as violating the equal protection clause of the Fourteenth Amendment).

[155] 42 U.S.C. § 1973ee-1(a).

[156] 19 U.S.C. § 794(a).

[157] The "purposes" section of the ADA does specifically reference voting: "[D]iscrimination against individuals with disabilities persists in such critical areas as employment, housing, public accommodations, education, transportation, communication, recreation, institutionalization, health services, *voting*, and access to public services." 42 U.S.C. § 12101(a)(3).

[158] *See* New York v. County of Schoharie, 82 F. Supp. 2d 19, 25 (N.D.N.Y. 2000) (holding that accessibility to polling places qualifies as a "service, program, or activity"); *see also* Am. Ass'n of People with Disabilities v. Hood, 310 F. Supp. 2d 1226, 1234 (M.D. Fla. 2004).

[159] *See, e.g.*, New York ex rel Spitzer v. County of Schoarie, 82 F.Supp.2d 19 (N.D.N.Y. 2000) (County violated ADA by having habitually inaccessible polling places).

[160] *See* American Association of People with Disabilities v. Hood, 310 F.Supp.2d 1226 (M.D. Fla. 2004) (holding that Florida had violated Title II by purchasing voting system that was not readily accessible to people with disabilities without third-party assistance); *but see* American Association of People with Disabilities v. Shelley, 324 F.Supp.2d 1120 (C.D. Cal. 2004) (holding that Title II does not provide the right to a secret and independent vote for people with disabilities).

[161] *See* Doe v. Roe, 156 F.Supp. 35 (D. Me. 2001) (Maine disenfranchisement statute violated equal protection clause of Fourteenth Amendment).

[162] 42 U.S.C. §§ 15301-545

[163] *Id.* at § 15421(b).

[164] *Id.* at § 154481(a)(3)(A).

[165] The Title III definition of "privately owned place of public accommodation" includes (A) an inn, hotel, motel, or other place of lodging, except for an establishment located within a building that contains not more than five rooms for rent or hire and that is actually occupied by the proprietor of such establishment as the residence of such proprietor; (B) a restaurant, bar, or other establishment serving food or drink; (C) a motion picture house, theater, concert hall, stadium, or other place of exhibition or entertainment; (D) an auditorium, convention center, lecture hall, or other place of public gathering; (E) a bakery, grocery store, clothing store, hardware store, shopping center, or other sales or rental establishment; (F) a laundromat, dry-cleaner, bank, barber shop, beauty shop, travel service, shoe repair service, funeral parlor, gas station, office of an accountant or lawyer, pharmacy, insurance office, professional office of a health care provider, hospital, or other service establishment; (G) a terminal, depot, or other station used for specified public transportation; (H) a museum, library, gallery, or other place of public display or collection; (I) a park, zoo, amusement park, or other place of recreation; (J) a nursery, elementary, secondary, undergraduate, or postgraduate private school, or other place of education; (K) a day care center, senior citizen center, homeless shelter, food bank, adoption agency, or other social service center establishment; and (L) a gymnasium, health spa, bowling alley, golf course, or other place of exercise or recreation." 42 U.S.C. § 12181.

[166] 42 U.S.C. § 12182.

[167] 42 U.S.C. § 12182(b)(2)(a)(ii).

[168] *See* PGA Golf Tour v. Martin, 532 U.S. 661 (2001).

[169] *See* Montalvo v. Radcliffe, 167 F.3d 873, 874 (4th Cir. 1999) (holding that child with AIDS could not participate in karate class).

[170] *See* Anderson v. Little League Baseball, 794 F.Supp. 342 (D. Ariz. 1992) (holding that Little League Baseball falls within the ambit of Title III because they own, lease, or operate a place of public accommodation).

[171] 47 U.S.C. § 609 *et. seq.*

[172] *See* Paralyzed Veterans of America v. D.C. Arena L.P., 117 F.3d 579, 789 (D.C. 1997) (holding that arena that provided lines of sight over standees for 70% of its wheelchair seats was in accordance with ADA regulations); *but see* Caruso v. Blockbuster-Sony Music Entertainment Centre, 193 F.3d 730 (3d Cir. 1999) (holding that ADA did not require line of sight over standing spectators).

[173] *See* Lara v. Cinemark USA, Inc., 207 F.3d 783 (5th Cir. 2000) (holding that viewing angles for wheelchair seats do not need to be as comfortable as those offered to the general public); *but see* United States v. Hoyts Cinemas Corp., 256 F.Supp.2d 73 (D. Mass 2003) (holding that wheelchair seats must be integrated into stadium general stadium seating plan).

[174] Like Title III, the precise accessibility requirements are a function of whether the facility pre- or post-dates the ADA. Physical structures, or "facilities," that pre-dated the ADA must be readily accessible to and useable by individuals with disabilities, when viewed in their entirety. 28 C.F.R. § 150(a). New facilities and alterations of existing facilities must be designed and constructed in such a manner that the facility or part of the facility (or the alteration) is readily accessible to and usable by individuals with disabilities. 28 C.F.R. § 35.151(a), (b).

[175] *See* McPherson v. Michigan High School Athletic Association, 119 F.3d 453 (6th Cir. 1997) (holding that Association's eight-semester rule did not have to be modified even if it excluded student whose progress through high school was slowed by a learning disability); *but see* Washington v. Indiana High School Athletic Association, 181 F.3d 840, 852 (7th Cir. 1999) (holding opposite).

[176] *Available online at* <http://www.census.gov/acs/www/ >.

[177] *Available online at* <http://www.census.gov/dmd/www/products.html >.

[178] *Available online at* <http://www.bls.census.gov/cps/cpsmain.htm >.

[179] *Available online at* <http://www.cdc.gov/nchs/nhis.htm >.

[180] *Available online at* <http://www.cdc.gov/nchs/about/major/nhis_dis/nhis_dis.htm>.

[181] *Available online at* <http://www.bls.census.gov/sipp/ >.

[182] *Available online at* <http://www.ilr.cornell.edu/edi/ >.

[183] *Id.*

[184] *Available online at* <http://www.ilr.cornell.edu/edi/c-statistics >.

[185] *Available online at* http://www.ilr.cornell.edu/edi/disabilitystatistics/>.

[186] *Available online at* <http://www.ilr.cornell.edu/edi/disabilitystatistics/StatusReports/2006-PDF/2006-StatusReport_US.pdf?CFID=24863415&CFTOKEN=95078547 >.

[187] *Available online at* <http://www.ilr.cornell.edu/edi/lsvrsp/Application/Index.cfm?CFID=24863415&CFTOKEN=95078547 >.

[188] *Available online at* <http://dsc.ucsf.edu/main.php >.

[189] *Available online at* <http://www.colemaninstitute.org/Research/RERCdescription.php>.

[190] Among other tasks, the chair of NIDRR heads the Interagency Committee on Disability Research which directs information exchanges on disability research activities among some seventy member agencies, which in turn may fund disability-specific data collection and analysis. *Available online at* <http://www.icdr.us/ >.

[191] *Available online at* <http://www.disabilityresearch.rutgers.edu/ >.

[192] *Available online at* <http://psidonline.isr.umich.edu/>.

[193] For instance, the United States Department of Labor, Office of Disability Employment Policy, sponsors the Job Accommodation Network housed at the University of West Virginia, *available online at* <http://www.jan.wvu.edu/>.

[194] DHHS, 45 CFR 46.101.a, 2008.

[195] 45 C.F.R. 46.101, Subpart D.

[196] The State Department posts these human rights reports on its website, *available online at* <http://www.state.gov/g/drl/rls/hrrpt/ >.

[197] *Id.*

[198] *See* Fourth Annual Report on the Implementation of the USAID Disability Policy, *available online at:* <http://pdf.dec.org/pdf docs/PDACF599.pdf >.

[199] *See* U.S. Agency for International Development, *USAID Disability Policy Paper* (1997) *available at* <http://pdf.dec.org/pdf_docs/PDABQ631.pdf>. *See also* U.S. Agency for International Development, *USAID Disability Policy – Assistance* (2004), *available online at* <http://www.usaid.gov/about_usaid/disability>; U.S. Agency for International Development, USAID Acquisition and Assistance Disability Policy Directive (2004), *available online at* <http://www.usaid.gov/about_usaid/disability/>; U.S. Agency for International Development, *USAID Acquisition and Assistance Policy Directive (Disability Policy on New Construction)* (2005), *available at* <http://www.usaid.gov/about_usaid/ disability/>.

[200] 42 U.S.C. § 2000e-5(d).

[201] 29 C.F.R. § 1601.20

[202] 29 C.F.R. §1601.27.

[203] *See* EEOC v. Caterpillar, 409 F.3d 831, 833 (7th Cir. 2005) ("EEOC is not confined to claims typified by those of the charging party.") (quoting Gen. Tel. Co. v. EEOC, 446 U.S. 318, 331 (1980).

[204] 42 U.S.C. § 12133.

[205] 541 U.S. 509 (2004).

[206] *See* Duvall v. County of Kitsap, 260 F.3d 1124, 1139 (9th Cir. 2001).

[207] 536 U.S. 181 (2002).

[208] 28 C.F.R. § 35.170(b).

[209] *Id.* § 35.170(b).

[210] 42 U.S.C. § 12188(a).

[211] 42 U.S.C. § 12188(b)(1)(B).

[212] *Id.* § 12188(b)(2)(A).

[213] *Id.* § 12188(b)(2)(C).

[214] *See* Sch. Comm. of Town of Burlington v. Dept. of Educ., 471 U.S. 359, 369 (1985).

[215] *See, e.g.*, Lester H. v. Gilhool, 916 F.2d 865, 873 (3d Cir. 1990); Jefferson County Bd. of Educ. v. Breen, 853 F.2d 853, 857-58 (11th Cir. 1988); Miener v. State of Missouri, 800 F.2d 749, 753 (8th Cir. 1986).

[216] *See* Sellers v. Sch. Bd. of City of Manassas, 141 F.3d 524, 529-32 (4th Cir. 1998); *see also* Crocker v. Tenn. Secondary Sch. Athletic Ass'n, 980 F.2d 382, 386-87 (6th Cir. 1992); Charlie F. v. Bd. of Educ. of Skokie Sch. Dist. 68, 98 F.3d 989, 991 (7th Cir. 1996); Heidemann v. Rother, 84 F.3d 1021, 1033 (8th Cir. 1996); Witte v. Clark County Sch. Dist., 197 F.3d 1271, 1275 (9th Cir. 1999); Padilla v. Sch. Dist. No. 1, 233 F.3d 1268, 1273 (10th Cir. 2000); Ortega v. Bibb County School Dist., 397 F.3d 1321, 1325 (2005).

[217] *See* W.B. v. Matula, 67 F.3d 484, 495 (3d Cir. 1995); *see also* Salley v. St. Tammany Parish Sch. Bd., 57 F.3d 458, 466 (5th Cir. 1995) (nominal damages); Quackenbush v. Johnson City Sch. Dist., 716 F.2d 141, 148 (2d Cir. 1983); see also Polera v. Bd. of Educ. of Newburgh, 288 F.3d 478, 483-86 (2d Cir. 2002) (monetary damages would not be available even if plaintiff had not failed to exhaust administrative remedies, nonetheless, available under § 1983 for IDEA violation).

[218] 20 U.S.C. § 1415(i)(3)(B) (2000).

[219] *Id.* § 1415(i)(3)(C).

[220] *Id.* § 1415(i)(3)(D)(ii).

[221] *See* Arlington Central School District Board of Education v. Murphy, 126 S.Ct. 2455 (2006).

[222] 42 U.S.C. § 15481 (2004).

[223] *See* Federal Defendants' Opposition to Plaintiff's Motion for Preliminary Injunction, 2006 WL 1505602, *2 (arguing HAVA confers no private right of action) in Taylor v. Onorato, 428 F.Supp.2d 384 (W.D. Pa. 2006) (holding that private plaintiffs have no private right of action HAVA access provisions).
[224] 42 U.S.C. 15511 (2004).
[225] 42 U.S.C. §§ 1997 *et. seq.*
[226] *See* 42 U.S.C. § 3613.
[227] *Id.* at § 3613(b).
[228] *Id.* at § 3613(c)(1).
[229] *Id.* at § 3613(e).
[230] *See* 42 U.S.C. § 3612.
[231] *See id.* § 3612(p).

INDEX

C

D

E

I

J

K

L

M

Q

R

S

Z